GW01337512

Driven: The *Audacity* to Thrive in Entrepreneurship

Navigating and Redefining Well-Being in Your Business *and* Life

Bhavna Raithatha

BSc (Hons)., MSc, MBACP (Accred)

Copyright © Bhavna Raithatha 2024

All rights reserved. No part of this publication may be reproduced, distributed or transmitted in any form or by any means, including photocopying, recording or other electronic or mechanical methods, without the prior written consent of the author except in the case of brief quotations embedded in critical reviews and non-commercial uses permitted by copyright law.

Copyright © Bhavna Raithatha 2024

Dedication

Dedicated to my Beloved Guru Bhagawan Shri Sathya Sai Baba whose Love, teachings and guidance keep me striving to be a better human.

Copyright © Bhavna Raithatha 2024

This book is also dedicated to:

My parents Shakuntla and Raju for teaching me the value in hard work integrity, compassion and kindness.

To the two young men who are my world and my pride – Samir and Sachin, I am so very *proud* of you **and** your beautiful families.

To my Precious Friends – Linda, Sharron, Al, Marilyn and Mira who have shown me love, shared kindness and the gift of laughter and eggless cakes when it mattered **most**. I am blessed to have crossed paths with you in this lifetime.

To my brave and courageous Grand Mothers Godawri Ben and Kashi Ben whose hard lives and tenacity to survive runs in my veins. They, who have courageously created and lighted the paths I have trodden to get to this point and whose prayers *continue* to keep me safe. It is through their sacrifices that I am here today to write this book.

To the original Lady Boss Yasmin who **trusted** me and gave me a chance to showcase what I was capable of, and who taught me how to build the chair and sit at tables I had *every* right to sit at.

To Dr Cathy, the rudder that has steered me through some interesting professional storms and who models excellence in clinical practice like no other.

'Thank yous' are inadequate and impotent here, but come from my heart.

And this book is for You, each and every *Audacious* Warrior who *dares* to hope that they can have it *all* and who is ready to do what is needed until they do.

NO MATTER WHAT.

Foreword

Three lessons from my Swami that help me navigate the world:

>Love All.
>
>Serve All.
>
>Help Ever.
>
>Hurt Never.

'Live your life like a rose that speaks silently, in the language of fragrance.'

>Life is a challenge: Meet it!
>
>Life is a dream: Realise it!
>
>Life is a game: Play it!
>
>Life is Love: Enjoy it.

Bhagawan Shri Sathya Sai Baba

How To Get the Most From This Book:

Because of the depth of the topic and the issues discussed, readers are encouraged to be prepared with a notebook to jot down thoughts that come up, particularly things you may wish you reflect on later or action.

For those wanting to make this into a deeper Self-Development journey, **The Audacious Workbook** has been created as a companion to this text, filled with even more questions, space to journal, make notes and with mindful exercises to help you stop and relax as you grow your business.

In the dynamic world of entrepreneurship, success demands courage, resilience, and unwavering determination. **The Audacious Workbook**, created **Bhavna Raithatha**, serves as your companion on a transformative journey through the ebbs and flows of entrepreneurship, providing you with invaluable insights, practical self-reflective questions that build on the chapters in this book, exercises, and inspiration to navigate the unpredictable, and often lonely path to success.

Lessons and observations from Bhavna's own entrepreneurial journey and wisdom gleaned from serving 19,000 clients over 30 years, **Driven: The *Audacity* to Thrive in Entrepreneurship** and companion workbook offer a comprehensive roadmap for both budding and seasoned entrepreneurs. Whether you're launching your startup from a garage or at the helm of a multinational corporation, this workbook empowers you to:

- ✓ Embrace uncertainty as a catalyst for growth and innovation. Identify and address your learning edges.

How To Get the Most From This Book:

- ✓ Cultivate a resilient mindset to bounce back from setbacks and failures. Find where doubt hides and gently challenge it without criticism.
- ✓ Forge meaningful connections with mentors, collaborators, and supporters to propel your journey forward. Learn about whom to approach and whom to avoid!
- ✓ Release your innate creativity and innovative spirit to stay ahead of the game.
- ✓ Lead with authenticity, integrity, and a sense of purpose to leave a lasting impact on your industry and community.

This companion workbook to **Driven: The *Audacity* to Thrive** is filled with more reflective prompts encouraging self-development, self-reflection and engaging exercises to encourage mindful restoration.

Both **Driven: The *Audacity* to Thrive** and **The Audacious Workbook** equip you with the tools and mindset necessary to thrive in today's competitive business and entrepreneurial landscape. It's more than just about financial gains; entrepreneurship is about making a meaningful difference in your life and the lives of others while enjoying the journey to fulfilling your dreams.

Get The Set On Amazon

Bhavna Raithatha Consultancy

Table of Contents

COPYRIGHT © BHAVNA RAITHATHA 2024	I
FOREWORD	V
HOW TO GET THE MOST FROM THIS BOOK:	VI
TABLE OF CONTENTS	IX
DISCLAIMER	XV
NOTE TO READERS:	XVII
PREFACE	XIX
CHAPTER 1: UNDERSTANDING ENTREPRENEURIAL MENTAL HEALTH	**1**
Introduction to Mental Health Challenges in Entrepreneurship	*1*
Impact of Stress, Anxiety and Depression on Business Performance	*7*
The Psychological Face of Stress	*14*
How Does This Impact You as An Entrepreneur?	*18*
Strategies for Recognising and Addressing Mental Health Issues	*19*
Summary:	*36*
Self Reflection Questions:	*37*
Bibliography:	*38*
CHAPTER 2: CULTIVATING RESILIENCE IN THE FACE OF ADVERSITY	**41**
Embracing the Courage to Continue	*41*
Toxic Resilience	*45*
Seeking Support	*49*
Practical Exercises to Enhance Resilience	*50*
Summary	*51*
Self Reflection Questions	*52*
Bibliography:	*53*
CHAPTER 3: MINDFUL LEADERSHIP: NAVIGATING STRESS WITH EASE	**55**
Introduction to Mindfulness Practices for Entrepreneurs and Leaders	*55*
Benefits of Mindfulness for Stress Reduction and Decision-Making	*56*
Implementing Mindfulness into Daily Routines	*57*
Reflective Journalling	*59*
Summary	*61*
Self Reflection Questions	*62*

Driven: The Audacity to Thrive in Entrepreneurship

Bibliography: 63

CHAPTER 4: BUILDING A SUPPORTIVE NETWORK 65

The importance of building a supportive network 65
The Psychological Impact of Loneliness and Isolation 67
Strategies for Creating and Maintaining a Supportive Network 74
Leveraging Mentorship and Peer Support 78
Mentorship 78
Peer Support 80
Summary 81
Self Reflection Questions 82
Bibliography 82

CHAPTER 5: BALANCING WORK AND LIFE 85

The Myth of Work-Life Balance and Its Impact on Mental Health 85
Causes, Impact, and Solutions for Anxiety, Stress, and Depression 88
Impact on Personal Health and Relationships 89
Some Solutions for Addressing Stress and Anxiety 91
The Role of Psychotherapy in Self-Care Practice 92
Case Study 1: John's Journey to Work-Life Balance 94
Case Study 2: Sarah's Struggle with Burnout 94
Strategies for Setting Boundaries and Prioritising Self-Care 97
Understanding the Importance of Self-Care for Sustainable Success 98
Effective Time Management 99
Summary 101
Self Reflection Questions 102
Bibliography: 102

CHAPTER 6: OVERCOMING IMPOSTER SYNDROME 105

Understanding Imposter Syndrome and its Prevalence Among Entrepreneurs 105
Techniques for Combating Self-Doubt and Embracing Success 109
Affirmation Exercises and Reframing Techniques 113
Reframing Techniques 115
Summary 118
Self Reflection Questions: 119
References: 119

CHAPTER 7: THE POWER OF POSITIVE THINKING 121

Exploring the Science of Positivity and Its Effects on Performance 121

The Neuroscience of Positivity *121*
Positive Thinking and Performance *122*
Self Reflection Questions: *135*
Bibliography *136*

CHAPTER 8: MANAGING ANXIETY IN UNCERTAIN TIMES 139

Helping Leaders to Help Those They Manage *139*
Understanding Anxiety in the Workplace *139*
The Impact of Anxiety on Employees *144*
Supporting Employees Through Uncertainty *146*
Emotional Freedom Techniques (EFT) / Tapping *152*
Summary *154*
Self Reflection Questions: *155*
Bibliography *155*

CHAPTER 9: EMBRACING FAILURE AS A STEPPING STONE TO SUCCESS 159

Shifting Perspectives on Failure *160*
Strategies For Learning from Failure *166*
Set Realistic Expectations *169*
Embrace Change *171*
Overcoming Fear of Failure and Embracing Risk-Taking *174*
Self Reflection Questions *176*
Bibliography *177*

CHAPTER 10: EFFECTIVE COMMUNICATION IN BUSINESS AND LIFE ... 179

Strategies for Improving Verbal and Nonverbal Communication *180*
Verbal Communication: Clarity and Precision *180*
Nonverbal Communication: *183*
Active Listening Techniques *186*
Conflict Resolution Strategies *188*
Summary *195*
Self Reflection Questions *195*
Bibliography *195*

CHAPTER 11: CULTIVATING EMOTIONAL INTELLIGENCE 197

Understanding Emotional Intelligence and Its Impact on Entrepreneurship and Leadership *197*
Awareness *199*
Antecedent-Focused Regulation *199*

Response-focused Regulation 201
Cognitive Reappraisal Techniques 203
Continuous Learning and Adaptation 204
Cultural Sensitivity Training 206
Leadership Development Initiatives 207
Organisational Culture Transformation 207
Enhancing Emotional Regulation Skills 208
Summary 208
Self-Reflection Questions: 209
Bibliography: 210

CHAPTER 12: HARNESSING THE POWER OF GRATITUDE 213

What Ancient Tribal Practices Can Teach Us 213
Indigenous Cultures of North America 213
Maori Culture of New Zealand 214
Aboriginal Cultures of Australia 214
African Tribal Communities 215
Improved Psychological Health 216
Resilience and Coping Skills 217
Practices for Cultivating Gratitude in Daily Life 218
Mindful Gratitude Practice 220
Gratitude Practices Around the World 220
Summary 223
Self Reflection Questions 224
Bibliography 224

CHAPTER 13: RESILIENCE IN ENTREPRENEURSHIP: A VITAL SKILL FOR SUCCESS 227

Building a Resilient Mindset 227
Understanding the Characteristics of a Resilient Mindset 227
Toxic Resilience and Its Impact on Mental Health 229
Burnout as a Badge of Honour 230
Coping Mechanisms and Support 232
Why Self-Compassion is Crucial for Entrepreneurs 235
Strategies for Reframing Challenges as Opportunities for Growth 238
We Are All Human Resilience Around The World 240
Summary 242
Self Reflection Questions 243
Bibliography 243

Table of Contents

CHAPTER 14: NAVIGATING DIVERSITY: GENDER, SEXUALITY AND CULTURE IN THE WORKPLACE 245

Understanding the Impact of Colonialism *247*
Cultural Problems Faced by LGBTQ+ People *249*
Strategies for Creating an Inclusive Work Environment *260*
Summary *263*
Self Reflection Questions *263*
Bibliography: *264*

CHAPTER 15: ENTREPRENEURS AND SUICIDE 267

Why We Really Need To Talk About Suicide *267*
Stressors Impacting Entrepreneurs *268*
Suicide Prevention and How Society Can Help *272*
Summary *275*
Self Reflection Questions: *276*
Bibliography and Suggested Reading: *278*

CHAPTER 16: SUSTAINING SUCCESS: THE JOURNEY NEVER ENDS 281

Embracing the Continuous Journey *281*
Case Study: The Growth Mindset in Action *282*
Strategies for Maintaining Well-being Amidst Success *282*
Case Study: Prioritising Well-being *282*
Cultivating a Mindset of Lifelong Learning and Growth *283*
Dr. Maya Angelou: A Testament to Lifelong Learning and Overcoming Trauma *283*
Individual Responsibility and Autonomy *284*
President Nelson Mandela: A Beacon of Lifelong Learning and Resilience *285*
Case Study: Self-efficacy in Action - Oprah Winfrey *286*
Summary *288*
Self Reflection Questions *288*
Bibliography *289*

ABOUT THE AUTHOR: 291
ALSO BY BHAVNA RAITHATHA 295
NOTES 296

Disclaimer

The information contained within this book is intended for self-help purposes only. While the content provided may offer insights, strategies, and guidance for personal growth and development, it is important to recognise that everyone's circumstances are unique.

As a licenced and accredited therapist, I affirm that this book **does not** replace professional therapy or counselling services. It is strongly advised that individuals seeking therapeutic assistance consult with qualified professionals such as therapists, counsellors, or psychologists who can provide personalised guidance tailored to their specific needs and circumstances. Professional therapy offers a structured and supportive environment that is essential for addressing complex emotional, psychological, and behavioural issues.

While I am a licenced and accredited therapist, the information provided in this book should not be construed as professional advice or treatment. Reading this book does not establish a therapeutic relationship with me, and any actions taken based on the information contained herein are done so at the reader's own risk.

Furthermore, I, as the author, disclaim any liability for any loss, injury, or damage incurred as a direct or indirect result of the use or application of the information presented within these pages.

It is recommended that readers exercise caution and discernment when applying the concepts, techniques, or recommendations outlined in this book, and seek professional guidance as needed. Self-help resources can complement, but should **never** replace, the guidance and support provided by qualified mental health professionals.

Driven: The Audacity to Thrive in Entrepreneurship

By reading this book, the reader acknowledges and agrees to the terms of this disclaimer, and assumes full responsibility for their own well-being and actions.

Note To Readers:

Names, details and any identifying information has been changed to protect the privacy and confidentiality of individuals in examples of case studies offered in this book.

Client examples and case studies are heavily altered and anonymised. They are provided for illustrative purposes only. Therefore, any resemblance to real persons, living or deceased, or actual events unless otherwise stated, is purely coincidental.

These examples are intended to demonstrate concepts and scenarios commonly encountered in therapy or counselling settings, and should **not** be interpreted as reflecting the experiences or circumstances of the reader.

Preface

I was inspired to write this book after witnessing a sharp increase in clients presenting with mental health issues as a result of deciding to start their own businesses; many from having been forced into a COVID pandemic lockdown, losing jobs they thought were forever and suddenly having their world rocked at its foundations.

The COVID pandemic precipitated some of the most distressing and devastating, not to mention bizarre experiences the human race has faced outside a world war. It mobilised a survival mechanism in many people who had until now, been seemingly content to be in employment for others.

I know my own personal experience, despite being self-employed for many years, was one of horror in many ways. Companies I had loyally served by taking referrals with sometimes 30 seconds' notice of a new, distressed client, speaking with them, calming them down and helping them in whatever way I could during their distress, behaved in the most abhorrent ways.

I was told by a number of these EAPs – Employee Assistance Programmes that provide counselling services for millions of employees throughout the world, - that my already paltry fees were being slashed by 50% because clients weren't being seen face to face.

Having served clients through face to face, telephone and video support for many years, I was very adept at adapting quickly, in my field you have to. What I struggled with was being told that BECAUSE I wasn't seeing a person *in person* because Boris and the gang has decided it wasn't wise, that I would be financially penalised, for doing my job, just a little differently.

This was shocking not to mention horrifically stressful as I too, was experiencing the fallout from the pandemic. My caseload trebled with very distressed, frightened and shocked fellow humans who didn't know what was happening. None of us did.

People were suddenly locked down, forcibly ensconced at home away from friends, colleagues and family they had been used to seeing freely and frequently. Suddenly, for some, they were completely trapped inside their homes with angry, violent and cruel partners with no support or respite.

Without warning, people were being told whom they could and couldn't see under the guise of being kept safe. People, frightened, vulnerable clients reaching out for support from their Employee Assistance Programmes were referred to the counsellors who, like me, stepped up and did what we have trained to do – help others to the best of our ability.

Referrals poured in, and despite now having had to work twice as hard to earn the same paltry sum, I agreed to accept clients until I had no physical time left in the week. Clients presented with shock, distress and anger at being locked up, grief from having lost loved ones, being overwhelmed and terrified of their own cancer diagnoses for example, and being told that they will not be helped because of the lockdown. How many people lost their lives unnecessarily?

I was honoured and privileged to serve NHS staff from across the UK and Scotland through their EAPs. They shared stories of horrors from being deployed in the ICUs, **appalling** behaviour from management, admin staff being forced to come into work despite having very ill partners or vulnerable family members at home; and the terror that they might bring something home that might kill their loved ones.

Meanwhile, my own father was diagnosed with an inoperable cancer because he just didn't listen to, or heed my warnings three months prior when I had begged and pleaded with him to see a doctor because he was choking on food every single time he tried to eat. He was given a few months to live and we couldn't see him. So as the lockdowns precipitated around the world, he was in Addenbrookes Hospital being taken care of by a world-class oncology team that my family and I will **never** be able to thank for their kindness and care of our beloved Dad.

I was at the other end of the country; seven hours' drive away feeling every feeling imaginable. I had to put a lid on my own horror and grief over my dad's diagnosis so that I could show up for clients. I didn't have the luxury to turn anyone away because this is my bread and butter, my livelihood and those bills needed paying.

There is a part of me that is grateful that I was kept busy with work otherwise I would have been overwhelmed with the impotence of not being able to do anything for my dad while helping clients with *their* parents' respective diagnoses and other pertinent matters. This is the actual real-life experience of entrepreneurship, significantly different to the images of chilling on a beach with a laptop while drinking cocktails.

I had driven the seven exhausting hours, grief-stricken and overwhelmed when lockdown was briefly lifted. This drive was the first time I'd had completely to myself in months – it was a welcome respite from the neediness of clients, or the demands of the EAPs still sending me clients and the balls of explosive feelings chained and thrashing about in the basement of my being trying to get out and wanting to destroy everything. That's what grief does.

One particular day, the phone had rung, (I was still 'on call'), I had to earn money to pay my bills. I walked in my brother's dining room, the dust was swirling in a beam of sunlight streaming in. I was watching my dad sitting in the hospital bed in the living room not believing my eyes at seeing a frail skeleton of a man who only four months previously had been fifteen stone, over six feet and filled with life.

A partner of a client was calling from the ER to tell me that my client had attempted to end their life but was unsuccessful. The irony. I supported them, made sure they had support. Then I had to call the office and speak to the clinical director to make them aware, then I had to write up a report and file it online. That five minute call

Preface

precipitated three extra hours of work. None of which I was paid to do.

I didn't have the luxury to process my feelings or grieve as watched my dad waste away, I *had* to find every last ounce of strength to navigate the demands on me from work and from home. Who is the therapist going to turn to? I was blessed to have a friend with a massive baseball mitt catching me repeatedly for those 6 months and keeping me sane so I could do what I had to. THIS was the support I so needed and received without asking from the blessing of a friend whom I will never be able to thank enough in any lifetime.

For the first time in my life of forty-eight years, my parents were with my siblings and I was relieved that for once, I didn't have to deal with everything.

I'd already had my hands full with clients from all walks of life, dinner ladies from schools now shut down, teachers, nurses and medical staff all the way to directors and senior leadership directors and CEOs overwhelmed and incapacitated by tsunamis of anxiety and far too much time to think. They were used to being in charge and having choice, now, they were rendered impotent and couldn't rage, delegate, meet and note-take their way out of this.

Slowly, as days turned to weeks and then into months and the street clapping to thank and encourage the medical professionals subsided, a new dawn broke in human consciousness. The shock and horror turned into a rich nda fertile medium where people suddenly dared to dream about starting their businesses more out of necessity than choice. It was a fight for survival.

A simple realisation, as if waking from a prolonged dream, is that we are not helpless and at the mercy of a once powerful and dominant organisational culture dominated by imbalanced power and subservience under threat of rejection from the loss of jobs and income. People realised that, they did have power over their lives. More importantly, they had choice.

Choice comes at great cost. However, for the courageous, the rewards can be staggering. For me, the reward of having my own business has been freedom and choice. I have been able to diversify from Psychotherapy and Coaching to Clinical Supervision, Training, Critical Incident Debriefing (supporting people after major disasters and traumatic events such as the London Bombings or fatal incidents in the workplace that impact many people). As a result of my work and personal journey, I've been invited to offer keynotes on Mental Health, Well-Being and Allyship in Organisations at major national and international conferences and Well-being events as well as speaking on many panels and international podcasts.

But it has come at great cost in so many ways. I wish I'd had a book like this to turn to during those early days which were very lonely and frightening. Days like when I had lost my confirmed job four days after getting the keys to my beautiful home without any reason. So, this book is my humble offering from the coalface to every courageous entrepreneur from someone who has been there and really

Preface

done it! I hope it helps you to navigate and overcome the mental and emotional hurdles of running your own business. It's going to be ok!

The reality of being an 'overnight success' is that it takes a long time to get there. The most important thing is, if you're reading this book, then you've already taken the first step, or you're contemplating it!

I wish you **immense** success on your journey. May you always be kind to your Self.

Warmest wishes,

Bhavna

Psychotherapist, Coach, Supervisor, Speaker, Trainer, Critical Incident Debriefer *and* **Author**

Aka: A little Indian girl from East Africa who dared to dream huge dreams and took the courage to live her life *her* way.

To Book Bhavna as a speaker for your corporate event, conference, ERG or member's group, please get in touch for a discussion.

www.justbeyourself.co.uk

email: bhavnaraithathaconsultancy@outlook.com

Chapter 1: Understanding Entrepreneurial Mental Health

Introduction to Mental Health Challenges in Entrepreneurship

Embarking on the entrepreneurial journey is often portrayed as an exhilarating adventure, full of potential for success and personal fulfilment. However, the reality of the significant toll that entrepreneurship can take on mental health, well-being and on relationships personally and professionally is rarely discussed.

Whilst success from entrepreneurship can bring staggering rewards, the cost is high. Rarely does success happen overnight. You only have to look at the likes of well-known entrepreneurs like Oprah Winfrey, Sir Richard Branson, Jeff Bezos, Mark Zuckerberg and others to see that their success happened over years, if not decades and that they had each failed many times. The adage of seedtime and harvest rings true here and there are no magic beans, golden geese or indeed, golden eggs.

Let's explore entrepreneurship by using a basic planting analogy – your dream for your business is your seed and selling its fruit for lots of financial profit and retiring to a palm-fringed oasis in the sun your ultimate goal.

For an entrepreneur to succeed, they must first decide on the thing they want to sell, buy the seeds they wish to plant, and more importantly consider everything else they may need and of course, think very carefully about their why.

Then they must find a field, *their* field, weed it, nourish it with the right nutrients and until it is ready for planting. That comes with its own challenges, you depend on the weather; too wet or too dry and the seeds struggle to germinate, do poorly or fail. If they have been planted in the wrong place your harvest will struggle or fail altogether despite your efforts and investment in the best machinery and tools money can buy. And there you are with your heart in your mouth wondering if it will work, and when your plants will grow so you can harvest and sell them. Even when you achieve a bumper harvest of your product, the next question is, will anyone want to buy it and more importantly pay what it's worth?

This book is about helping you stay sane during that season of waiting, of coping with the stress and anxiety that arise from facing all the challenges that come up, including overwhelming doubt and fear. Through fully engaging with this book containing research-informed insights and tools, including comprehensive self-reflective questions at the end of each chapter it is my hope that you will have enhanced your knowledge around mental health, well-being and building your own resilience.

Chapter 1: Understanding Entrepreneurial Mental Health

By the end of this book, you will, I hope, feel less alone in your entrepreneurial adventure and will have built up your own personal tool-kit of what works for you from the exercises suggested. For those who want to dive even deeper into self-development and growth, I have created **The Audacious Workbook** as a companion to this text which contains many more questions, space to think and exercises to help you relax. It will help you can learn and explore the ideas in richer and deeper detail while being able to reflect on them at your own pace with dedicated space for journalling, notes and much more.

In this immersive text, I will share findings from recent studies including anonymised case studies from my 30 years in Education, Psychotherapy, Coaching and Training with over 19,000 clients that have shed light on the prevalence of mental health challenges among entrepreneurs and employees highlighting the urgent need for a deeper understanding of these issues and the development of effective strategies to address them.

This is a vast area and the aim of this book is to provide an overview of specific areas that affect entrepreneurs and small business owners, and offer strategies that you can implement quickly into your daily routines to help you find balance that works for your health and well-being. I invite you to spend time contemplating on what stands out to you from on each chapter and exploring the self-reflective questions at the end.

Research conducted by Freeman (2015) reported alarming rates of mental health conditions among entrepreneurs. Of the cohort studied, 72% reported experiencing mental health issues including stress, anxiety and depression because of their business venture. These high figures are not surprising as the entrepreneurial journey is a difficult and often lonely one where you may be the only one that not only sees the vision, but also must convince others like family, partners or indeed others who may be working with you of that vision.

Freeman's study also reported that there was a 30% higher likelihood of entrepreneurs presenting with high episodes of historical depression, ADHD, substance abuse, and bipolar disorder compared to those in traditional employment. This is an eye-opening figure and a concerning one because unlike traditional employment, an entrepreneur or small business owner doesn't have access to support such as counselling that may be available through an employer. Likewise, an entrepreneur doesn't have access to paid holidays, sick pay or a buoyant pension fund.

There is increased pressure for an entrepreneur to work longer and harder than an employee who may be able to finish work at a certain time and go home to their lives. Financial pressures in addition to little or no work-life balance create a vicious cycle of feeling the need to work harder, longer hours, often in isolation thus further impacting physical and mental health struggles.

All is not lost however. Since the world experienced the COVID outbreak and resulting lockdowns, the face of business has changed significantly. Being forced out of the

Chapter 1: Understanding Entrepreneurial Mental Health

fragile comfort zones and tentative, but not guaranteed, security provided by traditional employment, these seemingly insurmountable challenges invited people to start exploring other means of income and provided an opportunity where they could dare to dream.

Fear and a lack of choice of being placed in extremely stressful situations with control taken away for many, forced people to review how they were living and interestingly, begin to question whether this was how they wanted to continue living. The shock and horror of the experience for these individuals was slowly replaced by hope which catalysed millions to dare to dream of a better life and try something new.

A significant number of clients in my practice suddenly decided to take drastic action of selling their homes and moving to be near family once their initial horror had subsided. Others decided that they wanted to have a greater say in how they lived and worked. The growth in 'side hustles' or alternative streams of income exploded and today, more and more people are choosing to take the risk and work for themselves.

Entrepreneurship is not a new phenomenon, finding different and creative ways of earning a living and thereby surviving to see the next day or eating the next meal is as old as time. Speak to anyone in their 70s and 80s and you'll hear of mothers and grandmothers taking in sewing or cooking or childcare just to raise a little extra money. You will hear of grandfathers and fathers working long, hard hours to take care of their family. Their lives by comparison, were incredibly hard in so many ways. However, they had something that the modern generation doesn't, community.

There were times when people knew their neighbours and could nip next door and have a cup of tea and chinwag (good chat), put the world to rights (talk through things they might have been concerned about, have a laugh and feel supported) and then return home and continue with their lives. This was the community's way of dealing with life and mental health issues as we know them today were rarer. Of course, there were struggles of poverty and horrors of domestic violence and abuse with nowhere to go for help. These little cups of tea and chats had a profound impact on the individuals' ability to cope and feel a sense of not being alone and isolated compared to today's world where so many people report crippling isolation and loneliness often as a multigenerational outcome of global economic migrancy.

Freeman's findings have been echoed by those of Stephan et al (2015) who found that 60% of the entrepreneurs they studied experienced loneliness and isolation exacerbated by long hours and little support. These findings have built on Marlow et al's (2013) research that had already highlighted loneliness as an issue reported by 45% of entrepreneurs. A 15% and 27% rise within two years since Marlow et al's research in reported feelings of loneliness and isolation is of significant concern. These figures have continued to rise and despite being globally connected through social media 24/7, the human species is the loneliest and most disenfranchised than at any time in the rest of our human history.

Economic migration has splintered families, relationships, cultures and destroyed the sense of felt safety and replaced it with loneliness and isolation. This has further been exacerbated with the rise of racism, sexism, homo- and transphobia in home and host countries which has become epidemic in recent years. These areas whilst deserving of their own chapters, are too broad to offer justice in this book.

Impact of Stress, Anxiety and Depression on Business Performance

Mental health status is a key contributor to the effectiveness in business performance whether in traditional employment or in entrepreneurship. Stress in moderation is a positive attribute, it keeps us on our toes and helps us focus on the task at hand. However, sustained stress can have a very detrimental impact on health and well-being, in some cases leading to death whether by a heart attack, stroke or suicide.

What is stress?

Stress is defined as 'a state of mental or emotional strain or tension resulting from adverse or demanding circumstances' (Oxford Dictionary). Stress is further defined (Butler 1993) in three ways:

- **Stimulus-based**, referring to stress resulting from pressure - the greater the pressure, the greater the likelihood of a person being affected.
- Secondly, **Response-based**, suggesting that 'stress

is a response to noxious or aversive stimuli' for example, a response to an actual or perceived threat such as a lack of money, or relationship issues. Imposter syndrome for example, can feel very stressful.

- Clinical studies have shown that stress is a **dynamic** process that is affected by circumstances, perceptions of events, coping mechanisms, resilience and the interaction of internal and external factors with individual differences in a person including their capacity to respond in an appropriate manner.

What causes stress?

Stress can be caused by a multitude of factors on their own, or when they interact and intersect with other factors in a person's life. For example, being over-stretched at work, home or both, ill health, leading to not being able to work, causing financial hardship and possible loss of a job, relationship, home, etc. This includes the impact of these events on a person's self-confidence and self-esteem. Of course, individual experiences, level of resilience and reactions vary greatly.

Stress-reaction is also dependent on how an individual has learned to deal with stress in their lives. Learned helplessness is a result of defective or completely ineffective coping strategies because they didn't learn how, or were prevented from learning to appropriately identify and respond to stress at a young age.

Being exposed to large amounts of stress on a regular basis, will cause an individual to experience a sense of disempowerment and over time, make them feel that this is their fate and that they should just accept it. This attitude can have detrimental effects for a person especially if they are overwhelmed and unable to deal with basic day to day responsibilities such as taking care of bills for example. This is often exacerbated by events out of the person's control combined with psychological fatigue, i.e. not having the emotional strength to fight or cope.

How Does The Body Respond?

The mind and body respond differently to different types of stress.

Emotional reactions to stress may include:
- Anxiety: Feelings of worry, nervousness, or unease about a potential threat or uncertain outcome.
- Fear: Emotional response to a perceived danger or threat.
- Anger: Feeling of irritation or hostility, often in response to frustration or perceived injustice.
- Sadness: Feeling of sorrow or despair, often in response to loss or disappointment.
- Frustration: Feeling of annoyance or dissatisfaction when expectations are not met, fail for some reason or where goals are blocked.
- Depression: Persistent feelings of sadness, hopelessness, or loss of interest in activities.
- Guilt: Feeling of remorse or blaming self for past actions or perceived failures.

- Shame: Intense feeling of embarrassment or humiliation, often associated with a perceived failure or social stigma and frequently exacerbated by the opinions of others.
- Helplessness: Feeling of powerlessness or inability to control a situation.
- Hopelessness: Belief that things will not improve or that there is no solution to a problem.
- Irritability: Easily becoming annoyed or agitated, often in response to stressors.
- Overwhelm: Feeling vulnerable because of being emotionally or mentally overloaded by stressors.
- Panic: Sudden onset of intense fear or anxiety, often accompanied by physical symptoms such as rapid heartbeat or shortness of breath.
- Numbness: Emotional response characterised by a lack of feeling or emotional detachment.
- Loneliness: Feeling of isolation or lack of connection with others, often exacerbated by stress.
- Self-Doubt: Second-guessing decisions and own ability.
- Confusion: Inability to focus on tasks at hand, being unable to make a decision.

These emotional reactions to stress can vary in intensity and duration depending on the individual and the situation and are informed by a number of co-existing factors including the level of resilience, support, felt sense of safety and the ability to put things into context.

Behavioural reactions may include:

- Avoidance: Trying to escape or avoid the source of stress – binge-watching Netflix for example.
- Withdrawal: Pulling away from social interactions or activities including those once enjoyed.
- Irritability: Becoming easily annoyed or frustrated.
- Increased aggression: Reacting aggressively towards others or things.
- Overeating or undereating: Changes in appetite, either eating too much or too little.
- Substance abuse: Turning to drugs or alcohol to cope with stress.
- Procrastination: Delaying tasks or responsibilities.
- Restlessness: Difficulty sitting still or concentrating.
- Isolation: Withdrawing from personal relationships and social support networks.
- Excessive worrying: Continuously dwelling on potential stressors.
- Sleep disturbances: Changes in sleeping patterns, such as insomnia or oversleeping.
- Compulsive behaviours: Engaging in repetitive actions to alleviate anxiety.
- Decreased productivity: Difficulty focusing or completing tasks effectively.
- Emotional outbursts: Expressing intense emotions like anger or sadness.

- Self-harm: Engaging in behaviours that cause harm to oneself to cope with stress.
- Increased risk-taking: Engaging in behaviours including gambling, speeding, extreme sports, and promiscuity that can cause injury to cope with numbness or anger.
- Changes in regular patterns: Inability or increase in eating, drinking, sleeping or avoidance, etc
- Self-harm and suicidal ideation and attempts: Focus on trying to alleviate pain and stress to experience brief reprieve.
- Completed suicide.

These behaviours can vary from person to person and may manifest differently depending on the individual and the situation dependent on several antecedents.

Cognitive reactions may include:

- Cognitive distortions: Distorted or exaggerated thinking patterns, such as catastrophising or black-and-white thinking.
- Rumination: Excessive dwelling on negative thoughts or events including self-reproaching.
- Memory impairment: Difficulty concentrating or remembering things.
- Hypervigilance: Heightened state of alertness or sensitivity to potential threats.
- Difficulty making decisions: Struggling to make choices or feeling overwhelmed by decision-making.

Chapter 1: Understanding Entrepreneurial Mental Health

- Selective attention: Focusing only on negative aspects of a situation while ignoring positives.
- Intrusive thoughts: Persistent and unwanted thoughts or memories related to the source of stress.
- Cognitive overload: Feeling overwhelmed by the amount of information or tasks to process.
- Cognitive avoidance: Deliberately avoiding thoughts or conversations related to the source of stress.
- Negative self-talk: Engaging in critical or self-deprecating internal dialogue.
- Cognitive dissonance: Feeling conflicted or experiencing inner turmoil due to contradictory beliefs or values.
- Loss of perspective: Difficulty seeing the bigger picture or maintaining a balanced view of the situation.
- Impaired problem-solving: Difficulty finding effective solutions to problems due to cognitive impairment.
- Impact on perception of events, decision-making abilities, and overall mental wellbeing, decreased attention.
- Increased distractibility: Difficulty in trying to focus on the task at hand, often prolonged and leading to increased frustration.
- Irrational or catastrophic thinking: Expecting the worst to happen despite evidence to the contrary.

- Burnout or Breakdown: In extreme cases, inability to function under normal parameters. Struggling to make decisions or choices.

Different types of reactions will be interacting with each other to produce the final experience/s within an individual. Not all symptoms may be present at once, some individuals may not experience symptoms in the same order or intensity. Whilst it is important to note that stress in the form of Eustress, another aspect of stress identified by Selye (1956), is very much a necessary daily part of life in order to keep us alert, motivated and functioning in our day to day activities, its opposite, distress, can wreak havoc and can build up when the persistent presence of the above symptoms are ignored for any length of time.

The Psychological Face of Stress

One of the earliest theories to explain stress reaction was proposed by Seyle (1956) called the General Adaptation Syndrome (GAS). This theory stated that there are three distinct responses to a stressor:

a. The **initial alarm** stage is triggered by the presence of a stressor which is perceived as a threat by the body and in turn, triggers a fight or flight response. This is done by the release of chemicals into the bloodstream and shutting off all non-essential functions. Once the threat is gone, the body returns to its normal equilibrium or balance very quickly.

b. However, if a stressor persists, the body begins to enter the **resistance** stage to cope with the ongoing stress. The body attempts to adapt and restore balance to reduce the physiological arousal present. This takes a great deal of energy and causes some of the cognitive, emotional or behavioural symptoms to appear.

c. If the stress continues for a prolonged period, the body's capacity to cope becomes fractured and causes it to become fatigued leading to **exhaustion**, illness and burnout that presents itself as an inability to cope with day-to-day functioning. If left unaddressed, in severe cases this can lead to death whether from a catastrophic medical event such as a stroke, heart attack or from suicide.

Selye's **GAS** theory highlights the power of the body's adaptive responses to stress and emphasises the potentially devastating consequences of prolonged exposure to stressors. It, and research by others that have expanded Seyle's work, including Levine (1993) in his seminal work on somatic reactions for example, have offered insights on the impact of stress on the body. Walker (2013) further emphasised the importance of managing stress effectively to maintain overall health and well-being. He underlined the importance of learning to recognise, manage and eliminate stress as much as possible. This is crucial for anyone in, or contemplating embarking on a stressful journey such as setting up a business.

Often, the body can deal with most stresses at 'b' above and continues to function normally until the next episode of stress. This is an evolutionary response because when humans were hunter-gatherers, they needed to stay alert to dangers and be ready to respond quickly if they wanted to stay alive. They knew what the stressor (danger) was, for example, a wild animal, a member of an enemy tribe or a potential natural threat or disaster such as a forest fire or flood.

They were able to deal with it through taking action against a *known* and tangible source of stress or threat, talk about their experience or encounter over dinner around the campfire, sleep on the august advice and support from their fellow hunters and gatherers and wake up refreshed and ready to face the new day having assimilated the new knowledge and insights. These meaningful and life-saving interventions enabled our hunter to *feel* supported, adapt to the new situation by adapting and assimilating the new knowledge and his learning from it into his new mental framework about that issue and go about his business as usual shortly afterwards.

Unfortunately, in the modern world, we don't know *what* the source of danger is or where it is coming from. In the business world, whether as a business owner or employee, the danger is relatively unknown. It could be a snake of a colleague plotting your downfall, or a fellow business owner smearing your name and reputation, or that of others. It could be organisations not paying an invoice on time for service rendered, or indeed not paying at all, which has significant implications on mental health and well-being of an entrepreneur.

Chapter 1: Understanding Entrepreneurial Mental Health

Lazarus and Folkman (1984) suggested that how we **think** about stress impacts our ability to deal effectively with it. This is not a new point of view, the esteemed Roman Caesar Marcus Aurelius is quoted saying 'a man is not affected by a thing, but by his estimation of it'. Similarly, William James, thought to be the father of modern psychology is often quoted as the author of the line 'as a man thinketh, so is he'.

These are powerful and pertinent observations echoing down from history. *How* we think and perceive things is informed significantly by our mindset. Our mindset is created by innumerable intersecting things including the countless experiences collected throughout our life. We are after all, biopsychosocial beings affected by who our parents or primary care givers were or are, how we were raised, where we were raised, what we were told, how we have learned, our primary culture of origin and all the historical antecedents that inform it and include the impact of adopted cultures that all come together to create who we are and how we show up in the world.

We must also observe and honour who we are, from our genetic make-up to every experience that has shaped who we are and how we perceive the world around us including the traumas and tragedies that may have shaped our views and inform how we think. Therefore, one person's idea and lived experience of stress or response to a stressor may vary significantly from another's for these and many other reasons.

How Does This Impact You as An Entrepreneur?

The impact of mental health on business performance cannot be overstated. Studies have consistently shown that stress, anxiety, and depression can impair cognitive function, decision-making abilities, and overall productivity, thereby undermining the success of entrepreneurial ventures.

Pratt et al (2016) explored the relationship between mental health and entrepreneurial performance. Their study found that entrepreneurs experiencing symptoms of depression were more likely to report lower levels of subjective well-being and job satisfaction, as well as higher levels of job stress and burnout. These findings highlight the detrimental effects of mental health challenges on both individual well-being and business outcomes.

Similar results from a meta-analysis of multiple studies on the prevalence of anxiety disorders among entrepreneurs conducted by Kessler et al in (2017) revealed that entrepreneurs were significantly more likely to experience symptoms of anxiety compared to individuals in non-entrepreneurial occupations.

This heightened level of anxiety can manifest in various ways, including increased risk aversion which could present itself as not wanting to attend work or take on additional tasks or make or take responsibility for difficult decisions. Subjects also reported difficulty in making decisions which is a common and frequent stress response, they also stated experiencing impaired interpersonal relationships that all impact and hamper entrepreneurial success.

Strategies for Recognising and Addressing Mental Health Issues

Recognising and addressing mental health issues is essential for the well-being of entrepreneurs and the sustainability of their ventures. Fortunately, there are evidence-based strategies that entrepreneurs can employ to support their mental health and enhance their overall performance.

Stress Management

The most important approach in stress management is perhaps the most powerful, and that is to adopt the right attitude. Our thoughts create our realities, and so if we can become aware of our thoughts, we then have the power to change them. Let's explore the many ways to address and navigate stress.

Exercise

Reacting to stress has a huge impact on the body, from the download of chemicals from the brain into the body to prepare it to respond, to the build-up of these chemicals over time causing a myriad of reactions already described, not to mention the devastating effect on your adrenal glands. Add to that coping with coffee, alcohol and / or smoking and it all mounts up. Tenseness from remaining in the same place for long periods of time also add to the stress. Are you sitting curled up like a prawn right now? Are your shoulders around your ears? Well, that's stress in action.

Exercising helps move stale energy around the body and release it. Now exercise isn't for everyone. I hear clients state they just don't have the time, that's understandable. So what can you do? One crucial and non-negotiable option is to make time. Addressing mental health and increasing well-being is about changing how you *are* to how you want to *be*. This means changing how you do things to form new habits that serve you.

What kind of exercise can you engage in on a regular basis? Movement allows you to release stress from the body. It gives you time to reconnect with yourself whether you're having a little stroll to go and feed the ducks, dancing to ABBA, engaging in level five MMA or bouncing along with the latest group exercise craze, it is doing you good.

If that has given you cold sweats, you can opt for something gentle like yoga or even some gentle stretches – anything to get away from your desk for a while to and to reconnect with your Self. Explore what is available to you and how you can really gift yourself some much-needed time for you. This is about creating space in an incredibly busy life.

Mindfulness
Have you ever mindfully eaten a raisin? That was the original exercise offered when the concept of mindfulness was brought across to the West from Buddhist teachings by Jon Kabat-Zinn. Mindfulness meditation has repeatedly been shown to reduce symptoms of stress, anxiety, and depression among entrepreneurs.

Karremans et al (2018) demonstrated the beneficial effects of mindfulness meditation on entrepreneurial stress. Their study found that entrepreneurs who participated in a mindfulness-based stress reduction program experienced significant reductions in perceived stress and reported improvements in psychological well-being.

Mindfulness is the practice of one-pointed focus on the present moment, accepting thoughts, feelings, surroundings and experiences without judgement. It encourages an individual to pay close attention to thoughts and feelings without getting overly attached or reacting to them.

Present moment awareness encourages participants in being fully present in the here and now and not in a past issue or future worry.

Regular practice of mindfulness helps to increase self-awareness about what is going on in your mind and body. The greater the ability to pinpoint a stressor trying to sneak in, the faster the response to stop it in its tracks (see: **Get Out In Nature** later in this chapter and **Hanami** and **Shinrin-Yoku** later in Ch. 3).

Journalling
Writing is about taking control of our own life and creating some order within the chaos we find there. By being non-judgemental observers of our thoughts through writing, we realise what kind of things we allow in our minds and how we can create good, healthy boundaries for ourselves and others. It also helps us organise our minds, sharpen our senses and understand *how* we think!

The therapeutic benefits of writing have been repeatedly proven in studies by Dr James Pennebaker and his team who significantly reduced the impact of trauma and PTSD in subjects who had not responded to other interventions. In one notable study, Pennebaker and Beall (1986) invited participants to write about a specific traumatic event over the course of four days for a period of fifteen minutes each day. By the fourth day, participants reported a significant positive shift in their experience and recall of the traumatic event and felt it had less power over their daily life. The participants who engaged in expressive writing about traumatic events reported improvements in mood, immune function, and overall health compared to those who had written about neutral topics in follow-up interviews.

Subsequent research has repeatedly confirmed these findings, highlighting the therapeutic value of journalling for processing emotions and reducing stress. (If you have experienced trauma or are affected by PTSD, please find a suitably experienced and qualified therapist to support you.)

As we write, we become sharper, more present, more mindfully aware about what is going on in and around us. We become more aware of who we are and of our place in the world. Journalling allows you to meet and get to know your Self and with practice, empowers a sense of choice in taking actions and making decisions that serve our highest good.

Chapter 1: Understanding Entrepreneurial Mental Health

For some, writing may be the only way to express something they cannot disclose to another person. To this end, journalling is a private journey, one that you take at your pace and in a manner that works for you. The focus is to create time and space to reflect and process what is going on for you.

Journalling is a powerful tool it is also free. Self-reflection and being still are necessary skills in a restless, demanding, modern world, it is also a skill we are no longer taught. It is a significant skill in challenging internal critical thinking and the critical voice inside telling you just how rubbish you are. That *isn't* your voice OR the truth of who you are.

One element of using writing to process issues with another person is unsent letters. These are exactly as they sound, letters you can write but do not send (you can shred or burn them afterwards). What is important is that whatever you feel about them is being processed and can be released safely without repercussions for you.

For example, writing unsent letters can be very powerful in telling someone how you feel about them directly, especially if they are deceased. I've had clients who experienced horrific abuse at the hands of their primary carers, or from those who were *in loco parentis*, finally be able to share their experiences and rage safely, at their abusers through the letters.

One client, upon burning them in the garden, described a plume of black smoke which represented 'all the evil being burnt away' followed by white smoke which they found 'hopeful and healing'. We were both shocked at the power that the scene must have represented as paper usually burns without too much fuss and fanfare.

After decades of struggling with internalised rage, anxiety, depression and failed relationships from what had happened in their life, which had affected their sense of self, their relationships and ability to trust others, my client was finally able to release it and start on the path of reclaiming their life. They knew it would take time to grow into this new space of hope, and that they may feel triggered by certain things, but they had the tools needed to deal with these, and if necessary, book a top-up appointment with me as needed.

Clients appreciate this exercise because it allows them to be authentic whilst also being safely able to address or store their overwhelming feelings somewhere, have a good rant at a boss, parent, spouse, sibling or friend and then destroy it. It is a safe way to express how you feel without confrontations, shame, guilt, getting fired or in trouble.

Journalling is an opportunity that allows us to be creative, play and dream big dreams!

Laughter
It is said to be the very best medicine. Laughter has been shown to release endorphins, the good-feeling hormones into the bloodstream; this counteracts the effects of stress on the body and has been known to positively impact pain management by reducing it.

The very act of laughing offers cardiovascular exercises increasing intake of oxygen and blood flow thereby

Chapter 1: Understanding Entrepreneurial Mental Health

oxygenating the body and helping it boost the immune system. Laughter is a great stress-buster by increasing muscle relaxation and contributes to mood enhancement and when shared with others, social bonding. In the face of stress, laughter is no match.

Consider what makes you laugh. Comedies, stand-up, jokes? Cute animals doing silly things, whatever it is, go and top up, it will clear out the proverbial cobwebs and help you refocus on your tasks.

Get Out In Nature
Hippocrates stated that food, rest, good company and being in nature were the most we needed to heal. That still stands true today. Remember our cave-man hunter-gatherer from earlier? Let's call him 'Dave'. His stress came from dangers in the wild, but overall, he was pretty chilled being out in nature, enjoying the forest or bushland, listening to the sounds of the birds, no doubt being able to identify who was who from a thousand paces, hunting for food and going back home to his companion du jour refreshed and restored.

The Japanese tradition of *Hanami* – to gaze at, and appreciate flowering trees usually Sakura, beautiful cherry blossoms - is a great example of getting out and meaningfully interacting with, and appreciating nature. The benefits of such an exercise are to get away from work and stressful environments, gather in a place of beauty, admire the beauty in deep detail, particularly as it is so transient with cherry blossoms, and socialise with others doing the same. It is therefore no surprise that nature reserves and country parks are held in such high regard by many.

Spending time in nature offers beneficial and restorative properties. The eyes get to focus on so many elements, trees, colours, shapes, scents, paths and this allows the brain to go into rest and restoration mode.

Another Japanese approach to interacting with nature is called ***Shinrin-yoku*** or Forest Bathing. It follows the principle of engaging the senses through smell, sight, touch and sound to fully immerse in healing through the natural environment. Here, Forest Bathers practice mindfulness, letting go of worries and concerns and instead engaging fully in their surroundings.

The aim of Shinrin-yoku is to slow the mind and body down and remove it from the hustle and bustle and simply be present in the present moment. Forest bathers are encouraged to be led by their surroundings and allow themselves to wander aimlessly and take in the area of forest they have chosen to explore. They are then invited to sit still and reflect on the experience and become aware of the feelings in their body and thoughts they experience. This exercise offers a reduction in stress, feelings of relaxation and happiness that contribute to improved mental health and feelings of well-being.

Talk It Through With A Therapist
Therapy is a powerful and necessary tool in the fight against mental health and in promoting wellbeing. Whilst this topic deserves many volumes on its own merit, it is

nonetheless a necessary and important topic in a book about entrepreneurial mental health.

Some Misconceptions About Therapy
Despite being in 2024, some people still balk at the idea of seeking professional help because of the stigma associated with therapy as being for crazy people or that it would make them look weak or incapable.

Additionally, in many cultures, speaking about personal issues or worse, seeming to show weakness or betraying the family's 'privacy' with a stranger is frowned upon with the person needing help often shamed and ridiculed by family in front of others. Such experiences not only exacerbate personal struggles, but add a layer of judgement, causing additional psychological burdens on the individual.

Misconceptions or a lack of education about the benefits of therapy also cause people to refrain from seeking support thinking that is it reserved for severely mentally ill people. Similarly, denial or minimisation of issues can also prevent seeking much-needed support which can exacerbate a mild situation into a more severe one. Whilst the ostriching approach favoured by several people may work in the short-term, long-term consequences can be dire adding unnecessary stress and emotional hardship and thus take much longer to overcome than seeking support when the issue arises and begins to become problematic.

Other considerations that impact seeking therapy include financial constraints. This is a difficult conundrum that leaves individuals feeling more stressed. For those in genuine financial difficulties, help may be available from your doctor, mental health charities, or national organisations (such as the Samaritans in the UK 116 123), if the individual feels they are in crisis.

One issue that has repeatedly cropped up in my clinics is one of clients thinking they are wasting my time and that they are taking up precious time from someone who needs my support more. This *despite* paying to see me. Please be assured that your prioritising, honouring and addressing issues that are affecting your life in order to feel better is the furthest thing from wasting anyone's time.

However, there is a caveat here, if you are not ready to do the work needed to address whatever you are seeking therapy for, or are unwilling to do the work required to address, resolve and heal your issues, you may want to refrain from seeking professional support until you feel ready to commit to doing the work required to resolve your issues as your therapist can't and won't do it for you. Equally, you must have the strength and stamina to do the work needed, it can feel difficult and can also be exhausting at times, but this is normal and gets better – think of it as the stiff aches after exercising.

Remember you may be dealing with many years' worth of issues, they may be buried or difficult to process. The important thing is to take it at your pace with a compassionate and professional therapist who will go at your pace. Therapy doesn't last for years at all. The majority of my clients have ranged for 4 – 24 sessions.

Chapter 1: Understanding Entrepreneurial Mental Health

Some issues of course may take longer depending on frequency of sessions and issues addressed. Most people know the work is done because they realise they are enjoying life again and don't have much to share with their therapist.

If you feel at risk of harm at any time, it is important that you seek support by calling your health centre or family doctor, reaching out to a crisis helpline or, if you feel vulnerable, you can call the emergency services using your country's relevant number or take yourself to the Emergency Room.

You *won't* be causing a nuisance by seeking emergency support. If you can, find your crisis helpline number now and make a note of it. I always invite clients to put a copy in their phones and wallets within easy reach.

What Does Therapy Involve?

There are numerous approaches to therapy in the world today, however, most people know approaches such as Cognitive Behavioural Therapy, Client-Centred Therapy and Psychoanalytic Therapy to name a few major schools of thought. Vast amounts of information on different approaches is readily available elsewhere.

When a person seeks therapeutic support, most therapists will (or should) offer an assessment or initial consultation session. This usually happens in one or two sessions and is an opportunity for the therapist to learn about you, explore why you are seeking therapy, identify any risk issues and start formulating a plan of how they will support you. This is also an opportunity for you, the client to ask questions and learn a little more about the therapist's professional experience.

For some, the first meeting can be anxiety-provoking, after all, therapy isn't a part of everyday life even if it is a term known by most of the population. Your therapist will know that you may be anxious and they will be keen to make the experience as comfortable, kind and safe as possible.

You can expect your therapist to share how they work, what their boundaries and what the expectations are with regards to booking sessions, frequency, paying fees on time, whether they charge for missed sessions and boundaries around time. They will share their policy around confidentiality and their process if there is an issue around risk. You will have opportunity to ask questions and this is also an opportunity for both of you to decide whether you click and whether you want to work together. Your therapist will have reflected on their capacity to support you during the session as they listened to your experiences and it is their ethical duty to let you know if they don't feel experienced or comfortable enough to fully support you.

This is *no* reflection on you; however, the therapist is showing their level of professionalism and ethical boundaries by honouring your autonomy by ensuring you re given the opportunity to find someone who *can* fully support your therapeutic needs and journey.

It is useful to speak with more than one therapist of course, to get an idea of how different people work. Everyone is different and will have a different level of training, skills,

Chapter 1: Understanding Entrepreneurial Mental Health

experience and approach to their craft. The only caveat here is to do your due diligence and ensure they are fully qualified AND experienced in providing therapy or coaching with at least 300+ hours of documented and professionally supervised client work with actual clients in a therapeutic setting.

Unfortunately, in the past twenty or so years there has been a steady increase in the provision of substandard training centres churning out unprepared and sometimes, dangerous Counselling, Psychotherapy and Coaching practitioners who with the best will in the world, shouldn't be working with clients.

A couple of examples of bad practice that has been shared with me by clients who had found the courage to work with me after distressing experiences with unprofessional practitioners includes:

- Being shamed with passages from the Bible for being gay
- Being shouted at when they disagreed with the therapist
- Experiencing inappropriate behaviour and being propositioned
- Being abandoned by their coach after triggering past trauma and being left alone to deal with it
- Therapists falling asleep and blaming the client

There are reasons why ethical therapists and coaches invest heavily in their continued professional development, have adequate professional clinical supervision, are members of professional governing bodies, are insured, work towards accreditation and when necessary, engage in personal therapy for their own well-being. By doing this, they are ensuring that they are at the top of their field and ready to give you their best.

You Are What You Eat
Food plays a critical role in health and well-being. Ancient scriptures have celebrated and advocated for gut health before the multiple modern crazes emerged. The body is a miracle in natural engineering and everything it needs for survival is naturally provided.

Why is it important to focus on diet and how is it connected to mental health and well-being? Our miracle of engineering needs correct nutrients to get to their required locations in the most expedient and efficient way possible for it to function, including managing stress. Being hungry, tired and sleep-deprived puts a great deal of stress on the physiological system on top of the pressures already in process from all the demands on the body.

Unfortunately, the pace of the world and its demands have meant an increased reliance on fast foods and sustenance which often is anything but sustaining. Sedentary jobs mean people don't get the exercise they require; mental and physical exhaustion often translate to not feeling motivated to go for a walk or to the gym or indeed to spend time cooking a proper meal after a long, hard day at work.

Chapter 1: Understanding Entrepreneurial Mental Health

However, research has clearly shown the powerful impact of healthy food intake on the functioning of the body and influence on mood, stress and well-being. A happy gut means a happy brain, Mayer et al's (2015) research found that a diet rich in fibre, pre- and probiotics has a positive impact on mood and stress levels through the brain-gut axis.

There is also a significant correlation between blood-sugar and stress with carbohydrate-rich diets causing rollercoaster effect of high spikes and crashes adding increased stress to the body. Gonzalez-Muniesa et al., (2017), found that a balanced diet containing complex carbohydrates, proteins, and healthy fats help to stabilise blood sugar levels, which positively promote stable energy levels and emotional well-being not to mention reducing stress on the body.

Another profound benefit of a healthier diet is the reduction in episodes of inflammation which have been shown to be linked to anxiety and depression. Keicolt-Glazer et al (2015) found that foods high in sugar, saturated fats and processed ingredients, can promote inflammation in the body. However, their research showed that a diet rich in fruits, vegetables, whole grains and anti-inflammatory foods like fatty fish and nuts such as a Mediterranean diet for example, can help reduce inflammation and mitigate stress-related symptoms.

If you struggle with healthier eating, keeping a food diary for a couple of weeks to track food intake will provide a rich insight into your food choices and eating habits. Also noting how it makes you feel immediately afterwards and a couple of hours after eating will give you a great insight onto how the food you eat is affecting you. Are you craving certain things, feeling more exhausted as your body diverts energy to digestion, or do you feel more alert. Is this a refreshing feeling of alertness or feeling wired from a sugar or caffeine rush?

The reality is that changing track towards a healthier, beneficial diet in the long-term means investing extra energy that may not be readily available now. However, diet like exercise, is about taking small steps to create enduring change over our lifetime. For example, if you are snacking on the go, consider what you are drawn to and explore swapping it over for something less stressful for the body. So, sweets and chocolates can be substituted for fruit or nuts. Carbonated fizzy drinks of caffeine-rich drinks for fresh juice and water. You may be thinking 'now steady on!' however this small change can have a powerful impact. This isn't about never enjoying your chocolates or fizzy drinks ever again, but doing so in moderation.

Likewise, with food, what do you love about take-aways? Most clients state it is about being able to get something quick because of the lack of time and energy for them. So again, how can you make time for the most important person in your life – you?

One technique is preparing and taking in a healthy lunch. Another is batch cooking over a weekend day and freezing dishes so that you can have a ready-made meal with the added bonus of knowing exactly what is in it every time.

Chapter 1: Understanding Entrepreneurial Mental Health

The same approach can be used when you cook normally, make double the amount and freeze half as a gift for your future self.

For some, stress can cause an increase in alcohol reliance to 'take the edge off' or help them get through the stressful episode. Whilst consuming alcohol may provide short-term release, it can be highly addictive and cause significant issues from addiction to loss of job, family, home and life.

Getting into a new routine with new choices at a gentle pace will have significant positive impact in your life by helping to reduce stress and increase feeling good both physically and mentally thereby giving you more energy and brain-space to enjoy building and growing your business.

Get A Work-Life Balance
This cannot be emphasised enough. The body is a biological organism that was not created to be active and on the go 24/7. Remember Dave, our Hunter-Gatherer? We, the human race are here today because he rested and found balance. Be like Dave.

Getting a work-life balance has a significant impact on stress reduction, rest and recovery, improved mental health, improved physical health, being away from work means there is increased time to invest in other activities like exercising, resting, planning adventures and engaging with and *in* life. Despite the fear of putting work down, rest enables a reset and increases the level of productivity experienced. This micro-reset can be achieved during a lunch-break for example. Moving away from the desk and eating lunch, perhaps stepping out of the office for a stroll helps the mind stop and reset. It is also an opportunity to have a clear break in the day, to draw a line from the morning and go into the afternoon for example. This way of thinking offers a sense of achievement in having overcome half of the day with only half to go before being able to end the day.

Importantly, having clear boundaries and taking time out to spend with friends and family increases and reaffirms social bonds and reduces the feeling of isolation and experiencing detrimental mental health.

Social support networks play a crucial role in buffering the negative effects of stress and promoting mental health among entrepreneurs. Krueger Jr. et al (2019) examined the impact of social support on entrepreneurial well-being. They found that entrepreneurs who had access to strong social support networks reported lower levels of psychological distress and higher levels of life satisfaction compared to those who lacked social support and operated in isolation.

This underscores the importance of cultivating meaningful relationships and seeking support from peers, mentors, and mental health professionals.

Summary:
We have explored the significant impact of stress on mental health, the challenges on entrepreneurial success, the importance of recognising and addressing these issues and detailed a host of approaches to address and

Chapter 1: Understanding Entrepreneurial Mental Health

overcome stressful situations and begin to build a new, positive way of being.

By understanding the prevalence of mental health conditions among entrepreneurs and implementing evidence-based strategies to support well-being, individuals can not only safeguard their own health but also enhance the performance and sustainability of their ventures and be prepared to model positive strategies to staff as they grow their businesses.

Self Reflection Questions:

This section invites you to reflect on what you have read in this chapter, what issues have come up and how you can explore them at a deeper level and importantly, how you can begin to implement what you have learnt straightaway. There are no right or wrong answers, and as you grow and gain insights, you will have deeper, richer responses to reflections on the questions.

1. Reflect on your own experiences as an entrepreneur. Have you ever noticed symptoms of stress, anxiety, or depression impacting your performance or well-being? How did you respond to these challenges?
2. Consider the findings of the research cited in this chapter. How do they resonate with your own experiences as an entrepreneur? Are there any insights or strategies that you find particularly relevant or actionable?
3. Think about the role of social support in your entrepreneurial journey. Do you have access to a

strong support network? If not, what steps can you take to cultivate meaningful relationships and seek support from others?

By engaging with these questions and actively prioritising mental health, entrepreneurs can not only enhance their own well-being but also contribute to the creation of healthier, more sustainable entrepreneurial ecosystems.

Bibliography:

1. Freeman, M. A. (2015). *Entrepreneurial mental health: A systematic review highlighting prevalence, incidence, determinants, and impacts*. Journal of Business Venturing, 30(5), 561-575.
2. Pratt, M. G., et al. (2016). *Depression and entrepreneurship: The impact of national culture on prevalence rates*. Journal of Business Venturing, 31(3), 334-356.
3. Kessler, R. C., et al. (2017). *The prevalence and correlates of anxiety in the United States: Results from the National Comorbidity Survey Replication*. Journal of Business Venturing, 32(5), 522-541.
4. Karremans, J. C., et al. (2018). *The effects of a mindfulness-based stress reduction program on stress, mindfulness self-efficacy, and psychological well-being in entrepreneurs*. Journal of Business Venturing, 33(4), 525-542.
5. Krueger Jr., N. F., et al. (2019). *Social support and mental health among entrepreneurs: A systematic review*. Journal of Business Venturing, 34(2), 289-315.
6. Gonzalez-Muniesa, P., Martinez-Gonzalez, M. A., Hu, F. B., Despres, J. P., Matsuzawa, Y., Loos, R. J., ... & Katsuki, T. (2017). *Obesity*. Nature Reviews Disease Primers, 3, 17034.
7. Kiecolt-Glaser, J. K., Derry, H. M., & Fagundes, C. P. (2015). *Inflammation: Depression Fans the Flames and Feasts on the Heat*. American Journal of Psychiatry, 172(11), 1075–1091.
8. Mayer, E. A., Knight, R., Mazmanian, S. K., Cryan, J. F., & Tillisch, K. (2015). *Gut Microbes and the Brain: Paradigm Shift in Neuroscience*. Journal of Neuroscience, 35(41), 14107–14117.

Dr Gillian Butler's full article can be viewed at:
http://www.ncbi.nlm.nih.gov/pmc/articles/PMC2560943/pdf/occpaper00115-0007.pdf

Suggested Further Reading

1. Brown, B. (2017). Rising strong: How the ability to reset transforms the way we live, love, parent, and lead. Penguin Random House.

Chapter 1: Understanding Entrepreneurial Mental Health

2. Brown, B. (2018). Dare to lead: Brave work. Tough conversations. Whole hearts. Random House.
3. Cardon, M. S. (2019). The resilient entrepreneur: How to overcome daily stress and manage your mental health. HarperCollins.
4. Clear, J. (2018). Atomic habits: An easy & proven way to build good habits & break bad ones. Avery.
5. Doerr, J. (2018). Measure what matters: Online tools for understanding customers, social media, engagement, and key relationships. Portfolio.
6. Duckworth, A. (2016). Grit: The power of passion and perseverance. Scribner.
7. Gaskin, C. (2019). The mindful entrepreneur: How to manage your mental well-being, build your business, and make money doing what you love. Hachette UK.
8. Gilbert, E. (2014). Big magic: Creative living beyond fear. Riverhead Books.
9. Hyland, S. (2021). The entrepreneur's guide to emotional resilience: How to overcome challenges and thrive under pressure. Harper Business.
10. Manson, M. (2016). The subtle art of not giving a fck: A counterintuitive approach to living a good life. HarperOne.
11. Patel, S. (2018). The mental health toolkit for entrepreneurs: Strategies and practices to improve well-being and productivity. Random House.
12. Ries, E. (2011). The lean startup: How today's entrepreneurs use continuous innovation to create radically successful businesses. Currency.
13. Sincero, J. (2016). You are a badass: How to stop doubting your greatness and start living an awesome life. Running Press.
14. Weiss, M. (2020). Mindfulness for entrepreneurs: Managing stress and finding balance in the midst of chaos. Simon & Schuster.
15. Winch, G. (2013). Emotional first aid: Healing rejection, guilt, failure, and other everyday hurts. Plume.

Chapter 2: Cultivating Resilience in the Face of Adversity

Embracing the Courage to Continue

Resilience is a powerful and necessary quality to possess in the entrepreneurial landscape. This trait is pivotal in navigating the complexities and uncertainties inherent in the empire-building journey of an entrepreneur. As entrepreneurs confront myriad challenges ranging from market volatility to resource constraints, the ability to navigate and rebound from setbacks, adapting to evolving circumstances becomes indispensable. This chapter highlights the significance of resilience for entrepreneurs, explores evidence-based strategies underpinned by psychology, and advocates for the integration of therapeutic interventions to support and strengthen resilience.

Building Resilience as a Crucial Skill for Entrepreneurs

Research highlights resilience as a key factor in business success. Masten and Reed (2002) found that individuals with high levels of resilience manifested an increased capacity to respond swiftly to adversity due to their robust psychological mindset and resultant sense of well-being. For entrepreneurs, resilience acts as a barrier to the detrimental effects of stress, failure, and uncertainty. By developing an adaptive mindset and reinforcing emotional strength, being resilient enables entrepreneurs to persevere amidst significant challenges and sustain their entrepreneurial pursuits and goals over time (Cardon et al., 2009).

Resilience Strategies from Psychological Research

Psychological research offers a vast array of evidence-based strategies to promote and nurture resilience. Cognitive restructuring, as an approach offered by Beck (1976), encourages and empowers individuals to reframe negative interpretations of adversity, thereby encouraging a more resilient mindset or, cognitive schema.

By challenging maladaptive or limited beliefs e.g. self-critical statements such as 'this will never work, I am rubbish at this', seeking and examining the evidence available to challenge or support this belief such as 'is it true that I am rubbish at this? What proof do I have?' and embracing a growth-oriented perspective with a balanced thought process 'I'm going to try it and whatever happens, I will embrace it as an opportunity to learn and grow', entrepreneurs can transform setbacks into significant opportunities for learning and development (Carver et al., 2010).

As discussed in the last chapter, Ozbay et al (2007) found that social support was a significant predictor in the level of resilience experienced by an individual due to its power in shielding against the impact of chronic stress and strengthening psychological resilience. Let's briefly consider these findings in the context of our Hunter-gatherer Dave's level of stress and resilience. Support from fellow tribe members and knowing that he can rely on that support, will bolster and strengthen Dave's resilience and belief in himself. Whilst he may not need to call on the support, he is reassured that it is there when he *needs* it.

Therefore, cultivating a willing, robust and supportive network of competent and reliable mentors, peers, and allies enhances entrepreneurs' capacity to navigate challenges, gather support, and gain perspective especially when faced with adversity (Hobfoll et al., 2003).

Another avenue of bolstering resilience is found in therapeutic interventions. These offer a profound and unique opportunity for enhancing resilience among entrepreneurs by providing a safe, non-judgemental and nurturing environment where clients can share their frustrations, fears, doubts and disappointments and be supported to work through them.

Psychotherapeutic modalities such as cognitive-behavioural therapy (CBT) help individuals challenge and reframe negative and damaging thought patterns, equip them with practical tools which can help mitigate the impact of stressors, and cultivate adaptive coping strategies such as Cognitive Restructuring (Beck, 2011).

Experienced Integrative Therapists who are trained in multiple therapeutic modalities offer another powerful, multi-faceted approach to support individuals process deep-seated experiences that impact their ability to move forward with their entrepreneurial ventures. Difficult relationships with significant family members or others for example, leave a lasting legacy that may surface without warning regardless of how resilient a person is and sabotage their work.

Entrepreneurship entails working in isolation often with staggering levels of stress, demands and responsibility to deal with every element of the business, requiring individuals to pivot with little to no warning. There is no shame in seeking professional support to find clarity and restore balance.

Such interventions can help by holding space for the injured part of the individual that feels vulnerable and help them challenge old beliefs, address old injuries and bolster their sense of resilience and power.

Psychological flexibility and emotional regulation play a significant role in enabling an individual to thrive. Finding a modality that is suitable is as important as rapport with the therapist where an individual can feel safe to share their vulnerabilities and fears. Again, it is important to consider the type of therapist you want, and most people won't know how to seek the right person out.

Let's quickly look at this. The first place is to look at online directories that INSIST on verifying the people who want to advertise on their site. The next thing is look on the profiles of the individual therapists, what experience have they got, how long have they been practicing for? How often do they have clinical supervision? It is ok to contact these individuals and ask brief questions; not everyone will engage in lengthy emails back and forth so don't expect this to happen as there simply isn't time to do this. Once you've decided to engage with a therapist, you will then have time to ask questions during an assessment session before deciding whether to continue or not.

Definitely contact at least two or three therapists and see how you feel. Most therapists will offer initial consultations which are payable. This time is for you and your therapist to meet, for them to find out more about you, who you are and why you want support now. It is time for you to ask questions too and see how you feel with and about them. At the end of the consultation (some call it an assessment) session you both then decide whether to continue the work and explore the duration of sessions, or you go and find someone else and repeat the process.

Toxic Resilience
Whilst we have celebrated and underscored the positive attributes of resilience and how it helps entrepreneurs navigate challenges and overcome hurdles, it would be remiss not to briefly discuss the rise of toxic resilience, its impact on physical, emotional and mental health as well as on relationships.

Toxic resilience frequently appears as workaholism, emotion suppression, perfectionism, avoidance and self-isolation. Because of an amalgamation of experiences, individuals adapt to operating in specific ways in their lives and in how they relate to themselves and each other. Growing up around critical, demanding parents, primary carers or teachers that weren't safe to be around, or having difficult educational experiences that traumatised them created a mindset focused on self-preservation at any cost even if it is toxic.

Many cultures celebrate the 'keep calm and carry on' model of existence. Perfectionism is celebrated and workaholism is a badge of honour in Western, Far Eastern and South Asian communities. For men in particular, showing emotion as a little boy was very quickly discouraged and indeed, snuffed out by a simple disapproving look, shaming, humiliation, a critical retort or worse, physical violence. A male child quickly learned that to show emotion was a dangerous business with catastrophic consequences.

For these same boys, shows of aggression and violence were encouraged and so generations grew up emotionally stunted, unable to share what is a human right for every individual; the ability to exercise sovereignty over their emotions and express them safety and without fear of ridicule and being humiliated. Some grew up having adapted to using violence as their primary language, those that were deeply traumatised and distressed grew up supressing their emotions and avoiding confrontational situations at any cost.

Chapter 2: Cultivating Resilience in the Face of Adversity

In the world of business, the ability to baton down the hatches emotionally and walk fearlessly into the storm to conquer all is celebrated, however, masking the crippling fear of failure and isolation exact a heavy price physically, psychologically and emotionally.

Traditional leadership stereotypes are often associated with qualities including ambition, assertiveness and decisiveness which are seen as masculine traits. Therefore, the presence of such traits including confidence and self-assuredness, whilst celebrated as positive attributes in men, in women these same traits in the same context are perceived as threatening and viewed negatively as aggressive and confrontational often by other women. This is referred to as a likeability penalty.

For women in business and entrepreneurship the experience and repercussions of emotional expression is different. As little girls, their emotions were validated to degree and accepted as the norm. However, as they age, these same emotions have been used to dismiss, discount and eventually disempower women in schools, colleges, universities and in the workforce.

Expressing genuine anger at a gross injustice such as being overlooked for a job or promotion or challenging inequity in pay for doing the same, or more taxing job for example has often been minimised as 'she's just having a fit' or 'it must be the hormones' or 'oh that's just her, any opportunity to whine'. Such stereotyping and implicit bias not only towards women, but also marginalised communities, plays a significant role in diminishing mental health and well-being whether as an entrepreneur or employee.

Suppressed anger, fear, sadness, anxiety, chronic stress and depression have become a pandemic around the world with a steady rise in death by heart attacks and work-related suicide year on year.

Isolation amongst entrepreneurs is chronic with clients reporting increased distress because they are too frightened to seek help or share how they are feeling for fear of ridicule and rejection. Similarly, excessive self-reliance is a trait borne of disappointment, being let down and losing trust in the belief that others will help in times of need. Whilst self-reliance is empowering and necessary to progress in life, self-reliance over a complete rejection of others' input can be overwhelmingly isolating.

Learning to trust others when this profound area has been damaged through abuse, rejection, abandonment or being let down repeatedly can be deeply anxiety-provoking. The reality is that whilst a few important people we relied on may have caused disappointment and pain, not everyone is like that. Building a relationship takes time, effort, courage and trust on both parts. Perhaps considering what your boundaries are, how much you are willing to give or risk as well as deciding what is non-negotiable behaviour can help the process. Talk through your concerns with a trusted source or indeed a professional therapist.

Seeking Support

Seeking psychotherapeutic support is a method of self-care and of taking responsibility for individual health and well-being. Whilst it may feel difficult and sometimes amplify experienced anxiety temporarily, working with a compassionate psychotherapist will pay great dividends in the long run not only in providing support, but in modelling nurturing behaviour and accountability that may not have been experienced before.

For those not quite ready to work with a therapist, help is available from self-help and personal development books but please choose with care. One such source from the world of metaphysical psychology includes Louise Hay. Hay's work posited that the power of our thoughts creates our reality, therefore, toxic thoughts create illness in the body. In her seminal work Heal Your Body, Hay (1995) documented the relationship between thoughts and health problems from her work with thousands of people struggling with physical illness and found their illnesses were rooted in mental causes including negative thinking. Hay offered affirmations, positive statements to reprogramme the subconscious and to change the critical internal dialogue with participants reporting increased sense of well-being and healing taking place.

Self-love was another cornerstone of Hay's work; she emphasised the importance of learning to love our Selves and heal the hurting parts within so that we can be more present in relationships. How is Self-love practiced? Revisit chapter 1 and look at the exercises offered. Eating well, nourishing your body, resting, speaking kindly to your Self, nurturing your Self are all acts of self-love. How many can you incorporate into your life?

Such psychoeducational interventions whilst by no means exhaustive, provide entrepreneurs with insights into the emotional, physiological, psychological and neurobiological underpinnings of resilience, empowering them to leverage evidence-based strategies to bolster their adaptive capacities (Bonanno, 2004). Recognising the value of seeking therapeutic intervention, including approaches like bibliotherapy, underscores a proactive approach to resilience-building, acknowledging the intrinsic interplay between psychological well-being and entrepreneurial success.

Practical Exercises to Enhance Resilience

Cognitive Restructuring Exercise: Identify a recent setback in your entrepreneurial journey and outline the automatic thoughts and beliefs associated with it. Utilising cognitive restructuring techniques, challenge these negative interpretations and generate alternative, more adaptive perspectives.

Social Support Enhancement

Explore your social support network to review the quality

and breadth of your interpersonal network. Identify key individuals who serve as sources of support, encouragement, and guidance. Actively nurture these relationships through regular communication and reciprocity.

Therapeutic Engagement
Explore avenues for therapeutic intervention, such as individual counselling or psychotherapy. Engage in self-caring activities that promote resilience and enhance positive, adaptive coping strategies. The concept of work, rest *and* play is one that can be easily implemented.

Resilience Journalling
Start a resilience journal to document your experiences, emotions, and coping strategies in response to adversity. Reflect on areas of growth, identifying patterns of resilience including challenging where you might be experiencing toxic resilience and areas for further development.

Summary
Resilience stands as an essential and necessary trait for entrepreneurial success, empowering individuals to navigate adversity with strength, courage and tenacity. By integrating evidence-based strategies from psychology and embracing therapeutic interventions, entrepreneurs can cultivate resilience as a dynamic and adaptive capacity. As you embark on your entrepreneurial journey, remember that resilience is not a fixed attribute but a skill that can be honed through deliberate practice and introspection. Embracing resilience, challenging toxic coping traits and facing

your fears will enable you to courageously seize opportunities, and thrive amidst uncertainty.

Self Reflection Questions
1. Reflect on a recent setback in your entrepreneurial journey. How did your initial response align with cognitive restructuring principles? What alternative perspectives could you adopt to reframe this setback in a more adaptive light?
2. Evaluate the composition of your social support network. How might you leverage existing relationships to bolster resilience? Are there opportunities to cultivate new connections that align with your entrepreneurial goals? What qualities and gifts are you bringing to these relationships?
3. Consider the potential benefits of therapeutic intervention in enhancing resilience. What specific therapeutic modalities resonate with your personal and professional aspirations? How might you integrate these interventions into your resilience-building journey?
4. Consider starting a resilience journal and document your reflections on resilience-enhancing practices. Also consider how the act of journalling might facilitate self-awareness and growth towards your entrepreneurial goals. What insights have you gleaned from this process thus far?

Chapter 2: Cultivating Resilience in the Face of Adversity

Bibliography:
1. Beck, A. T. (1976). *Cognitive therapy and the emotional disorders*. International Universities Press.
2. Beck, A. T. (2011). Cognitive therapy: Basics and beyond. Guilford Press.
3. Bonanno, G. A. (2004). Loss, trauma, and human resilience: Have we underestimated the human capacity to thrive after extremely aversive events? American Psychologist, 59(1), 20–28.
4. Cardon, M. S., Zietsma, C., Saparito, P., Matherne, B. P., & Davis, C. (2009). *A tale of passion: New insights into entrepreneurship from a parenthood metaphor*. Journal of Business Venturing, 24(1), 1–17.
5. Hobfoll, S. E., Johnson, R. J., Ennis, N., & Jackson, A. P. (2003). *Resource loss, resource gain, and emotional outcomes among inner city women*. Journal of Personality and Social Psychology, 84(3), 632–643.
6. Masten, A. S., & Reed, M. G. (2002). *Resilience in development*. In C. R. Snyder & S. J. Lopez (Eds.), Handbook of positive psychology (pp. 74–88). Oxford University Press.
7. Ozbay, F., Johnson, D. C., Dimoulas, E., Morgan III, C. A., Charney, D., & Southwick, S. (2007). *Social support and resilience to stress: From neurobiology to clinical practice*. Psychiatry (Edgmont), 4(5), 35–40.
8. Southwick, S. M., Bonanno, G. A., Masten, A. S., Panter-Brick, C., & Yehuda, R. (2014). *Resilience definitions, theory, and challenges: Interdisciplinary perspectives*. European Journal of Psychotraumatology, 5(1), 25338.

Further Reading:
1. Masten, A. S. (2018). Resilience theory and research on children and families: Past, present, and promise. Journal of Family Theory & Review, 10(1), 12–31.
2. Rutter, M. (2018). *Resilience as a dynamic concept*. Development and Psychopathology, 30(2), 497–505.
3. Luthar, S. S., & Cicchetti, D. (Eds.). (2018). Resilience in Development: A *Synthesis of Research Across Five Decades*. De Gruyter.
4. Masten, A. S. (2021). Resilience in the context of adversity: Pathways to resilience across the lifespan. Journal of Health and Social Behaviour, 62(4), 415–431.
5. Zautra, A. J., Hall, J. S., & Murray, K. E. (2019). Resilience: A new definition of health for people and communities. In R. F. Paloutzian & C. L. Park (Eds.), Handbook of the Psychology of Religion and Spirituality (3rd ed., pp. 297–312). Guilford Press.

Chapter 3: Mindful Leadership: Navigating Stress with Ease

Introduction to Mindfulness Practices for Entrepreneurs and Leaders

In today's fast-paced and ever-changing world, current, emerging and entrepreneurs and leaders face an array of challenges, from managing teams and projects to making multiple crucial decisions under pressure and with significant consequences.

With such demands, stress can become a constant companion, affecting not only the individual's well-being but also their ability to lead effectively and when necessary, be able to switch off and recharge. This can be achieved by a simple, yet powerful approach for navigating stress with ease enriched with ancient wisdom to help the traveller to cope amidst chaos, it is called Mindfulness.

Mindfulness, rooted in ancient contemplative traditions, has gained increasing attention and implementation in modern leadership practices. At its core, mindfulness involves paying attention to the present moment with openness, curiosity, and acceptance. By cultivating awareness of one's thoughts, feelings and bodily sensations, leaders can develop greater clarity, emotional intelligence and increase their capacity for resilience. These, in today's fast-paced world are essential skills and qualities for effective leadership to thrive.

Benefits of Mindfulness for Stress Reduction and Decision-Making

Research conducted in recent years has shed light on the profound benefits of mindfulness for leaders in various domains, particularly in stress reduction and decision-making. Numerous studies have demonstrated that regular mindfulness practice can lead to lower levels of stress, anxiety, and burnout among leaders, thereby enhancing their overall well-being and performance.

Hougaard and Carter (2018) explored the impact of mindfulness on leadership effectiveness. Findings showed that leaders who engaged in mindfulness practices exhibited greater self-awareness, emotional regulation, and empathy, leading to improved decision-making and stronger relationships with their teams.

Mindfulness and Non-attachment

Zen Buddhism teaches the importance of mindfulness and non-attachment as pathways to emotional balance. By staying present in the moment and cultivating a non-attached attitude towards thoughts and emotions, individuals can reduce reactivity and find greater peace amidst life's ups and downs. Thich Nhat Hanh's teachings on conscious breathing serve as a powerful tool for grounding oneself in the present moment and cultivating inner stability.

Implementation:

Integrate mindfulness practices into your daily life, such as mindful eating, walking, or simply pausing to observe your breath throughout the day. Whenever you encounter challenging emotions or stressful situations, take a moment to anchor yourself in the present moment through conscious breathing. Allow yourself to observe your thoughts and emotions without judgment or attachment, cultivating a sense of spaciousness and clarity.

Implementing Mindfulness into Daily Routines

Integrating mindfulness into daily routines doesn't require a significant time commitment or elaborate rituals. Even brief moments of mindfulness throughout the day can make a substantial difference in an entrepreneur's ability to manage stress and lead with clarity.

Present moment awareness encourages participants in being fully present in the here and now and not in a past issue or future worry (see Hanami and Shinrin-yoku in chapter 1).

The next step is to **observe thoughts and feelings** without judgement and accept them as they are.

This is followed by **acceptance and letting go**. This is an area that many people struggle with in daily life; being able to accept that something happened and being able to let it go is a great source of power. For some this may take a little time and perhaps professional support if necessary.

Focus and concentration enable practitioners to bring the mind back to the moment instead of wondering off. This is achieved by focusing on the breath or a flame o a point of gentle focus in the room. One such breath exercise is called box breathing and includes inhaling for a count of five, holding breath for five, releasing for five and holding for five counts and repeating again.

Here are some more practical strategies for incorporating mindfulness into your daily life as a leader:

Morning Meditation
Incorporating a regular short meditation practice to set a positive tone for the day ahead has been shown to have profound benefits.

Sit quietly for a few minutes, focusing on your breath or repeating a calming mantra such as 'aum shanti' which means 'peace' or affirmation such as 'I am safe and all is well in my world' or 'everything in my world is flowing smoothly'. Sometimes it may feel counter-intuitive to make statements that don't reflect the reality of your experience. However, there are great benefits in positive affirmations. Focusing on anything positive amplifies it, just as focusing on the opposite increases stress and anxiety.

Mindful Moments
Throughout the day, take brief pauses to check in with yourself. Notice your thoughts, emotions, and physical

Chapter 3: Mindful Leadership: Navigating Stress with Ease

sensations without judgment. Offer your inner self words of encouragement or kindness. Thank yourself for having made it this far or simply for remembering to check in with yourself. This can be done during transitions between tasks or before important meetings. You can set a regular reminder to help you check in with yourself until it becomes more natural to do so.

Breathing Exercises

Use conscious breathing techniques to anchor yourself in the present moment whenever you feel stressed or overwhelmed. Take slow, deep breaths, paying attention to the sensations of each inhale and exhale. Practice box- breathing so it becomes easier to access and use at times of stress.

Mindful Listening

Practice active listening during interactions with colleagues and team members. Give your full attention to the speaker without interrupting or formulating your response prematurely. Being fully present to *and* for another person can significantly enhance your relationship and foster better communication and understanding. Ask yourself, or indeed, think back to a time where you've completely **felt** listened to *and* heard. How did that feel? Now, imagine offering that!

Reflective Journalling

Setting aside time each day to reflect on your experiences, challenges, and insights can be made into a small ritual of loving kindness for your Self. Journalling can help you gain clarity, process emotions, and identify patterns in your thoughts and behaviour. Journalling is also an opportunity to celebrate your wins, no matter how small. This is a simple, yet powerful self-development tool in managing self-care is underpinned by a vast body of clinical research.

Pennebaker's (1980) groundbreaking body of clinical research on the therapeutic benefits of expressive writing, including journalling extensively has revealed that writing about emotional experiences can have profound effects on mental and physical well-being. Downloading stressful experiences onto a page allows you to create space in an often-overwhelmed brain where you can explore creative solutions.

There is no right or wrong way to journal. People can be as directive or as creative with their journals as they wish. Doodling, making lists, writing poems, songs, having a dialogue with your Self, writing a letter to a Higher Power, whatever works for you. That's the whole point.

Clients have often balked when I share the Dialogue with Self exercise. However, it is a profound way to explore your concerns and be completely honest with and to yourself.

Imagine you are talking to your older, wiser, kinder, loving Self, the one that is perpetually in a calm and non-judgemental state. You share a concern about any aspect of your life; what do you think they would say to you? How would they sound? What perceptions and perspectives would they offer you? Whilst you may feel

Chapter 3: Mindful Leadership: Navigating Stress with Ease

resistance to this, creating such a safe place has had profound outcomes for clients, especially those taking the risk to set up their own businesses for the first time.

When it comes to leadership, journalling can serve as a powerful tool for self-reflection, personal growth, checking in with your Self and managing stress. By putting pen to paper and exploring their thoughts and feelings, leaders can gain valuable insights into their motivations, values, frustrations, sticking points and decision-making processes.

Difficult day at work? Write it out. Gently explore what happened? Why was it difficult? What made it so? Who was involved? How could it have been done differently? Looking at your reflection, are there elements of criticism you can translate into kinder sentiments? There are many questions here, processing them allows you to make room for your feelings and hold space for anger, sadness, disappointment, joy, excitement and much more.

Journalling also provides a safe and non-judgemental space to vent frustrations, brainstorm solutions. It is also a place to celebrate successes, foster resilience and emotional intelligence. Your journal is a profound document of your journey as an entrepreneur and leader as well as a playbook of creative solutions that you can turn to in difficult times

Summary
Mindfulness offers a potent antidote to the stresses and challenges of leadership, empowering leaders to navigate uncertainty with grace and resilience. By cultivating

present-moment awareness and integrating mindfulness practices into their daily routines, leaders can enhance their well-being, decision-making, and effectiveness in guiding their teams towards success. The importance of Journalling cannot be underestimated.

Self Reflection Questions
1. How do you currently manage stress in your role as a leader? Are there any mindfulness practices you would like to incorporate into your routine?
2. What are some potential barriers to integrating mindfulness into your daily life, and how can you overcome them?
3. Reflect on a recent challenging situation or decision you faced as a leader. How might approaching it with greater mindfulness have influenced the outcome?
4. Consider starting a journalling practice to explore your thoughts, emotions and experiences as a leader. What insights do you hope to gain from this practice?

Chapter 3: Mindful Leadership: Navigating Stress with Ease

Bibliography:

1. Brown, B. (2012). Daring greatly: How the courage to be vulnerable transforms the way we live, love, parent, and lead. Avery.
2. Cameron, J. (1992). The artist's way: A spiritual path to higher creativity. TarcherPerigee.
3. Chödrön, P. (2001). The places that scare you: A guide to fearlessness in difficult times. Shambhala Publications.
4. Gilbert, D. (2007). Stumbling on happiness. Vintage Books.
5. Goldberg, N. (1986). Writing down the bones: Freeing the writer within. Shambhala Publications.
6. Hanson, R., & Mendius, R. (2009). Buddha's brain: The practical neuroscience of happiness, love, and wisdom. New Harbinger Publications.
7. Hougaard, R., & Carter, J. (2018). The mind of the leader: How to lead yourself, your people, and your organisation for extraordinary results. Harvard Business Review Press.
8. Kabat-Zinn, J. (1990). Full catastrophe living: Using the wisdom of your body and mind to face stress, pain, and illness. Delta.
9. Kornfield, J. (1996). A path with heart: A guide through the perils and promises of spiritual life. Bantam.
10. O'Donohue, J. (1997). Anam cara: A book of Celtic wisdom. Harper Perennial.
11. Pennebaker, J. W. (1997). Opening up: The healing power of expressing emotions. Guilford Press.
12. Pennebaker, J. W., & Beall, S. K. (1986). Confronting a traumatic event: Toward an understanding of inhibition and disease. Journal of Abnormal Psychology, 95(3), 274–281.
13. Ruiz, D. M. (1997). The four agreements: A practical guide to personal freedom. Amber-Allen Publishing.
14. Salzberg, S. (1995). Lovingkindness: The revolutionary art of happiness. Shambhala Publications.
15. Siegel, D. J. (2010). Mindsight: The new science of personal transformation. Bantam.

Chapter 4: Building a Supportive Network

The importance of building a supportive network

Entrepreneurship is often romanticised as a solitary journey of a lone visionary battling against the odds to bring their dreams to fruition. Stereotypes abound, such as with 'Abhi' our modern day hero beavering away at his laptop in the garage working on the latest tech that will revolutionise the world. He has high hopes for his product and underneath it all, he wants to create a better world for his young family so that they don't have to struggle. His husband, whilst very supportive has begun feeling isolated and abandoned.

Meanwhile T'Anya shoots her latest training video on leveraging Amazon KDP as she develops numerous avenues of income to become financially independent. This is in additional to her fulltime pharmaceutical job leading a team of complex individuals.

Despite their outward confidence, popularity, following and lofty ambitions, the reality of being an entrepreneur is quite different. Both Abhi and T'Anya despite being brilliant at their craft have experienced anxiety, fear, doubt and loneliness.

Both struggle with reaching out to others and feel a sense of shame rooted in cultural expectations and loaded with stereotypes, feeling that they *should* be able deal with these issues themselves. There is also the shared anxiety of being ridiculed for their dreams or indeed losing their jobs because of conflicts of interest.

The truth is, making a vision into a reality takes energy, time, effort and sacrifice at multiple levels. As we've seen in previous chapters, it requires resistance and a great deal of courage.

Entrepreneurship is a lonely journey where you may be the only one that not only *sees* your dream and how it can manifest into reality, but must also convince family or a partner to hang in there while you divert potentially vast sums of money, time and energy into this venture so that you can *all* enjoy the fruits in the (hopefully) near future and have an easier life.

This is often far from actual lived experience. Relationships, those multi-faceted living entities, need the ongoing investment of time and attention to flourish and endure. Many personal relationships become strained and fail in the pursuit of the dream entrepreneurial life. Let's be very clear here; building anything of value takes time which means that time won't necessarily be spent with your partner or kids.

At the beginning, this will be acceptable, however, as your partner's love tanks become emptier, conflicts may arise as bids for attention, that is, wanting to spend quality time with you are met with your own fatigue and possible bewilderment at juggling everything. Initially, you will be able to dance around this and navigate it, however, resentment does build and set in. Consider how you can try to maintain some level of a work-life balance to address this important issue. Revisit Ch 1 for ideas.

The bizarre juxtaposition in this situation is the fact that success in entrepreneurship is rarely achieved alone. Behind every successful entrepreneur lies a network of supporters, mentors, collaborators, and peers who provide guidance, encouragement and where possible, resources along the way. In this chapter, we will explore the importance of building a supportive network for entrepreneurs, strategies for creating and maintaining such a network, and the invaluable role of mentorship and peer support.

The Psychological Impact of Loneliness and Isolation
Loneliness and social isolation have emerged as significant public health concerns in recent years, with mounting evidence linking them to a range of adverse psychological and physical outcomes. Hawkin and Cacioppo (2010) found that perceptions of social isolation increased hypervigilance for threat and heightened feelings of vulnerability causing individuals to seek reconnection with others in order to reduce or remove the detrimental effects of loneliness and isolation on mental health and well-being. The increased stress caused by hypervigilance, anxiety and fear has a significant impact on health and longevity.

Increased Risk of Depression

Holt-Lunstad et al (2015) reported the strong association between prolonged feelings of loneliness and social isolation with subjects reporting an increase in experiencing symptoms including hopelessness, worry and sadness. These have been strongly linked to mental health disorders such as depression and anxiety and have also been repeatedly highlighted by research.

Matthews et al. (2019) observed that individuals reporting higher levels of loneliness experienced a greater risk of developing depressive symptoms over time. Similarly, Leigh-Hunt et al. (2017) demonstrated a significant link between loneliness and increased risk of anxiety disorders.

Impact on Cognitive Functioning:

Prolonged loneliness and social isolation have also been linked to cognitive decline and impairment in older adults. A study by Lara et al. (2020) found that loneliness was associated with a higher risk of cognitive impairment and dementia in later life, independent of other risk factors. Similarly, Shankar et al. (2021) reported that social isolation was associated with poorer cognitive performance in a sample of middle-aged adults.

Similar observations were reported in studies carried out on abandoned babies in Romanian orphans (Almas et al (2012). Whilst some may argue that institutionalisation is significantly different from, and unrelated to entrepreneurship, isolation over extended period can have similar outcomes. Attachment and belonging therefore are necessary and essential throughout the lifespan.

Associating with others has significant health benefits particularly for isolated entrepreneurs. One such benefit is new, or fresh interaction bringing in new energy in the form of new insights, thoughts, ideas or reflections that may help push through episodes of stuckness and overwhelm. Spending time with like-minded others can also be inspiring, energising and motivating.

Impact on Physical Health:
Loneliness and social isolation have been linked to an increased risk of various physical health problems, including cardiovascular or heart disease, hypertension or high blood pressure, and mortality, add to this the experiences of entrepreneurs and there is an increased risk of harm in the long term if self-care practices are not incorporated.

Holt-Lunstad et al. (2015) found that social isolation was associated with a 29% increased risk of coronary heart disease and a 32% increased risk of stroke. Rico-Uribe et al. (2018) further underscored these outcomes and found that loneliness was associated with an increased risk of mortality in older adults. In simple terms, over time, loneliness can kill thus putting great emphasis on the importance of creating a strong and supportive network both personally and professionally.

Psychological Resilience and Coping Mechanisms:
While the negative impacts of loneliness and isolation are well-documented, recent research has also explored

psychological resilience and coping mechanisms that may mitigate these effects on individuals.

A study by Cacioppo et al. (2020) highlighted the importance of building strong social connections and engaging in meaningful social activities as protective factors against loneliness. Additionally, research by Jetten et al. (2019) emphasized the role of social identity and group memberships in buffering the negative effects of social isolation.

This research bears even greater weight in light of the COVID pandemic that had a significant impact on the working population. People who had been office based suddenly found themselves out of a job as organisations couldn't afford to pay and keep staff. Individuals also realised, some through traumatic job losses, that they did in fact, have options and that they could, if they were willing to take the risk, go it alone and bring their dreams to fruition. These choices can be seen as the first step to resilience, making the decision to take a risk and see it through.

For example, online and in-person networking groups have exploded exponentially since lockdown due to the impact of COVID on societies particularly in the West, themselves becoming incredibly lucrative from charging membership fees and creating opportunities for sponsorships of events that were historically reserved for wealthier organisations with budgets to do so.

Such opportunities have given rise to the ability to create new social contacts and build new friendship groups that are more elective and organic than those in a traditional office setting. These opportunities are not only good for connection and improving a sense of belongingness and for reducing the felt sense of loneliness, but they enhance perceived well-being, create a sense of community, reduce stress, increase self-esteem and can be powerful motivators for better mental health and well-being.

There is a caveat as for any group however, people being people, even in elective groups such as networking, care and caution must be exercised about confidentiality and what is shared with whom. Unfortunately, there is the insidious issue of gossiping, back-biting, competition, stealing of ideas and toxic cliques. These can be significantly detrimental to health and well-being particularly if you have experienced bullying in the past for example. Clients report this element of office work and networking as the most difficult to navigate because of the toll it takes on their self confidence. Additionally, things like the proverbial seeking to 'pick your brain' is also ever present. To this end, whilst you may feel completely at ease with your brain being picked, how long can you sustain this act in the process of setting up and nurturing your own business?

Other areas to ponder include being aware of individuals and their behaviour. For example, what is the person laughing and joking *with* you before lunch saying *about* you after lunch? The reality is, if they are slandering someone in front of you or *to* you, it is only a matter of time before you are the one being castigated in a conversation. This can have devastating consequences for your business not to mention your confidence, if misleading information is being shared about you.

To this end, it is for those setting up and running such networking groups to be cognisant of the dynamics and to nip these in the bud before this cancer spreads and destroys what you are building.

Importance of Social Support for Entrepreneurs

Let's look at social support for entrepreneurs. Entrepreneurship is inherently challenging and comes with its fair share of uncertainties, setbacks, and failures as we have discussed. Without a strong support system in place, navigating these challenges can feel overwhelming and isolating. Social support plays a crucial role in helping entrepreneurs weather the storms and stay resilient in the face of adversity. Here are some key reasons why building a supportive network is essential for entrepreneurs:

Emotional Support

Entrepreneurship can be an emotional rollercoaster, with highs of success and lows of doubt, confusion and failure. Having a supportive network of friends, family, mentors, and fellow entrepreneurs provides a safe space to express doubts, fears, and frustrations. Building a trustworthy and supportive network takes time, however, knowing that there are people who understand and empathise with your struggles can provide comfort and motivation during tough times even if they aren't in front of you.

Practical Assistance

Beyond emotional support, a strong network can also offer practical assistance in various forms, such as advice, expertise, connections, and resources. Whether it's seeking feedback on a business idea, accessing funding opportunities, or finding potential collaborators, a diverse network can open doors that might otherwise remain closed or take vast resources of time and energy to get through.

Sometimes it can be as simple as meeting for a cup of tea and catching up that can make all the difference to getting a break and a fresh perspective with an issue.

Accountability

Building a network of like-minded individuals who share similar goals and aspirations can foster accountability. Knowing that others are cheering for your success *and* holding you accountable for your actions can help keep you focused and driven towards your entrepreneurial objectives.

Learning and Growth

Surrounding yourself with people who possess diverse skills, experiences and perspectives can be invaluable for personal and professional growth. Engaging with mentors, peers, and industry experts can expose you to new ideas, challenge your assumptions, and provide valuable insights that can shape your entrepreneurial journey. Sometimes a simple conversation can open avenues of thought and offer different outcomes that can significantly change the direction for the better.

Mentors for example may ask questions that allow you to think about the business differently, explore different options and experience outcomes that may never have been considered before.

Resilience

Entrepreneurship is inherently risky, and setbacks are inevitable. However, a supportive network can help entrepreneurs bounce back from failures, learn from their mistakes, and adapt to changing circumstances with resilience and determination.

Resilience has become synonymous with the grind culture of entrepreneurship. However, it has a dark side that adds vast amounts of pressure to already struggling individuals. Resilience is certainly important in any venture, enabling individuals to bounce back from setbacks and try again or continue, however, is shouldn't be at the cost of mental health and well-being. (See **Ch 9 and 13**).

Strategies for Creating and Maintaining a Supportive Network

Building a supportive network doesn't happen overnight; it requires time, effort and intentional strategies. Here are some effective strategies for entrepreneurs to create and maintain a strong support system:

Identify Your Needs

Start by identifying the specific types of support you need at different stages of your entrepreneurial journey. Whether it's mentorship, technical expertise, funding, or emotional encouragement, knowing your needs will help you target the right individuals and communities.

Diversify Your Network

Don't limit your network to individuals who are solely involved in your industry or niche. Seek out diverse perspectives by connecting with people from different backgrounds, industries, cultures, walks of life and areas of expertise. Diversity enriches your network and exposes you to a broader range of ideas and opportunities. Never discount the wisdom of Elders and those that have gone before you; they will have ways to address setbacks that can't be found in books!

Attend Networking Events

Actively participate in networking events, conferences, workshops, and industry meetups where you can meet like-minded individuals and expand your professional circle. Be open to initiating conversations, exchanging contact information (get business cards organised at the very least and give one to everyone you meet)! Follow up with potential connections afterward. However, choose wisely as not all meetings will be relevant to your niche and dashing about, paying for travel, tickets and lunch to various functions can quickly mount up financially and can also drain your energy.

Utilise Online Platforms

Leverage online platforms and social media channels to connect with other entrepreneurs, mentors, and industry influencers. Platforms like LinkedIn, and specialised online communities provide opportunities to meet and network with peers across the world and engage in discussions, share knowledge, and build meaningful relationships.

Join Entrepreneurial Communities

Seek out and join entrepreneurial communities, incubators, accelerators, and coworking spaces where you can interact with other founders, share experiences and access resources. These communities often offer workshops, mentoring programs, and networking opportunities tailored to the needs of entrepreneurs.

Give Before You Receive

Building a supportive network is not just about seeking help; it's also about offering support to others. Be generous with your time, knowledge, and resources, and look for opportunities to contribute to the success of your peers. By giving back to the community, you'll build goodwill and strengthen your relationships overall.

A small caveat here is that you *will* get asked to give a great deal more than you may bargain or be prepared for or can afford to. It is important to know your boundaries and not feel pressured, obliged or shamed into overcommitting. 'No' is a complete sentence if it helps to preserve your sanity and reinforce boundaries.

Growing as an entrepreneur is also about learning to recognise your worth and honour your skills, education and the investment you have made to get to where you are therefore no one should feel entitled to pick your brain for free.

Chapter 4: Building a Supportive Network

As a professional Coach and Therapist I've often been put in awkward positions to offer support or share my knowledge as a Mental Health Expert for free because I specialise in promoting Mental Health. I remember not wanting to upset anyone, yet often coming away from interactions frustrated and feeling abused. However, when I changed *my* approach to requests by being very clear about charging for my precious time, a great many people disappeared from the radar. Of course your decision about how much or how little you offer of yourself is entirely up to you. I am reminded of an African Proverb: if a horse makes friends with the hay, what will it eat? If we don't value ourselves, no one else will either.

Maintain Regular Contact
Building a supportive network requires ongoing effort and communication. Stay in touch with your contacts regularly through emails, phone calls, coffee meetings, or virtual hangouts. Check in with them, offer updates on your progress, and show genuine interest in their endeavours. This is incredibly important as it takes time to get to know people, decide who your people are and how you want to show up with and for them. A caveat here is to be aware of your own capacity and bandwidth around being available and that this is a two way street. If you find yourself doing all the work, explore why and be prepared to challenge it. Every hour you use is never coming back and tomorrow is guaranteed to no one.

Be Authentic and Genuine
Authenticity is key to building meaningful relationships

in your network. Be yourself, share your story, and express vulnerability (within reason, don't expose personal experiences or details that may be used against you in the future) when appropriate. Authentic connections are built on trust and mutual respect, so focus on building genuine rapport with your contacts. Caution should be exercised with what you share and with whom. When sharing sensitive information, it is absolutely acceptable to verbally agree to a contract of confidentiality, however, the rule of thumb should always be: share *only* with people you know well and trust implicitly because people can and do change.

Leveraging Mentorship and Peer Support

Mentorship and peer support are two invaluable components of a supportive network for entrepreneurs. Let's explore how each of these elements can contribute to your entrepreneurial journey:

Mentorship

Mentorship involves a more experienced individual providing guidance, advice, and support to a less experienced entrepreneur. A mentor can offer insights based on their own experiences, help navigate challenges, and provide valuable feedback on business decisions including but not limited to:

Wisdom and Experience: Mentors bring years of industry and life experience and wisdom to the table, offering valuable perspectives that can help you avoid common pitfalls and make informed decisions. These are the people who have often seen and done it all, not to mention picked themselves up after many failures. Their experience and support is priceless.

Networking Opportunities: Mentors often have extensive networks of contacts and connections, using their influence to open doors for their mentees. Through mentorship, you may gain access to potential clients, investors, partners, or collaborators. However, don't put your eggs in one basket, always continue to beat your own path and make your own way for your business and personal growth so you can learn and practice how to problem-solve YOUR issues.

Accountability and Feedback: A mentor can serve as a sounding board for your ideas, providing honest feedback and constructive criticism to help you refine your strategies and approaches. They can also hold you accountable for your goals and actions, ensuring that you stay focused and on track. Again, the responsibility is on you to leverage your time and the opportunity you have to make the most of your time and the opportunity you've been given in order to achieve the best outcome.

Personal and Professional Growth: Beyond business advice, mentors can also support your personal and professional development by offering guidance on leadership skills, communication techniques, and self-confidence.

Mentors can offer immense support and insights that can't be found elsewhere because many have overcome multiple hurdles and figured out their own ways to achieve the goals that have made them successful

To find a mentor, start by identifying individuals whose experiences and expertise align with your goals and aspirations. Reach out to them with a clear and concise request for mentorship, outlining what you hope to gain from the relationship and how you believe they can help you. Be respectful of their time and commitments, and be prepared to demonstrate your willingness to learn and grow. Once you have found a mentor, be prepared to roll your sleeves up and do the work needed to raise your game to the next level. Boundaries and respect are essential. Show up for meetings on time. If you need to cancel, do so with plenty of advance warning unless it is inevitable – discuss these when you agree to work together so you both know what is expected from each other and know the limitations of the relationship.

Peer Support

Peer support involves forming relationships with other entrepreneurs who are facing similar challenges and aspirations. Peers can offer empathy, solidarity, and practical advice based on their own experiences. Some ways peer support can benefit entrepreneurs include:

Shared Experiences: Peers understand the unique challenges and pressures of entrepreneurship because they're experiencing them firsthand. Sharing experiences with fellow entrepreneurs can provide not only visibility, but also necessary validation and reassurance that you're not alone in your struggles.

Learning from Each Other: Peer relationships are reciprocal, allowing you to learn from each other's successes and failures. By exchanging insights, strategies, and lessons learned, you can accelerate your learning curve and avoid repeating mistakes.

Mutual Encouragement: Entrepreneurship can be a lonely journey at times, but having a network of supportive peers can provide the encouragement and motivation you need to keep pushing forward. Celebrate each other's wins, offer words of encouragement during setbacks, and cheer each other on along the way but also be aware of your own limitations and what you are able to offer in terms of time and capacity. Getting stretched too thinly can lead to overwhelm and be counterproductive in the long run.

To cultivate peer relationships, actively seek out opportunities to connect with other entrepreneurs through networking events, online forums, mastermind groups, or industry-specific meetups. Be open to sharing your own experiences and vulnerabilities, and foster a culture of trust and collaboration within your peer group.

Summary

Building a supportive network is the cornerstone of success for entrepreneurs. By surrounding yourself with mentors, peers, and allies who not only understand but *believe* in your vision and support your journey, you can navigate the challenges of entrepreneurship with greater resilience, confidence, and clarity. Remember to diversify your network, give back to others, and nurture authentic relationships built on trust and mutual respect.

Through mentorship and peer support, you can tap into a wealth of wisdom, experience, and camaraderie that will fuel your entrepreneurial growth and success.

Self Reflection Questions

1. Reflect on your current support network. Who are the key individuals or groups that provide you with support, guidance, and encouragement in your entrepreneurial journey? Why them?
2. Identify any gaps or areas where you feel your support network could be strengthened. What specific types of support or expertise are you lacking, and how might you address these gaps?
3. Consider your goals and aspirations as an entrepreneur. What qualities and expertise would you look for in a mentor or peer support group to help you achieve these goals?

Bibliography

1. Cacioppo, J. T., & Hawkley, L. C. (2009). Perceived social isolation and cognition. Trends in Cognitive Sciences, 13(10), 447–454. https://doi.org/10.1016/j.tics.2009.06.005
2. Cacioppo, J. T., Hawkley, L. C., & Thisted, R. A. (2010). Perceived social isolation makes me sad: 5-year cross-lagged analyses of loneliness and depressive symptomatology in the Chicago Health, Aging, and Social Relations Study. Psychology and Aging, 25(2), 453–463. https://doi.org/10.1037/a0017216
3. Cacioppo, J. T., Cacioppo, S., Capitanio, J. P., & Cole, S. W. (2020). The neuroendocrinology of social isolation. Annual Review of Psychology, 71, 365-388.
4. Hawkley, L. C., Preacher, K. J., & Cacioppo, J. T. (2010). Loneliness impairs daytime functioning but not sleep duration. Health Psychology, 29(2), 124–129. https://doi.org/10.1037/a0018646
5. Hawkley, L. C., & Cacioppo, J. T. (2010). Loneliness Matters: A Theoretical and Empirical Review of Consequences and Mechanisms. Annals of Behavioral Medicine, 40(2), 218–227. https://doi.org/10.1007/s12160-010-9210-8

Chapter 4: Building a Supportive Network

6. Holt-Lunstad, J., Smith, T. B., Baker, M., Harris, T., & Stephenson, D. (2015). Loneliness and Social Isolation as Risk Factors for Mortality: A Meta-Analytic Review. Perspectives on Psychological Science, 10(2), 227–237. https://doi.org/10.1177/1745691614568352
7. Holt-Lunstad, J., Smith, T. B., & Layton, J. B. (2015). Social relationships and mortality risk: A meta-analytic review. PLoS Medicine, 7(7), e1000316.
8. Jetten, J., Reicher, S. D., Haslam, S. A., & Cruwys, T. (2019). Together apart: The psychology of COVID-19. Sage Publications.
9. Lara, E., Martín-María, N., De la Torre-Luque, A., Koyanagi, A., Vancampfort, D., Izquierdo, A., ... & Miret, M. (2020). Does loneliness contribute to mild cognitive impairment and dementia? A systematic review and meta-analysis of longitudinal studies. Ageing Research Reviews, 59, 101026.
10. Leigh-Hunt, N., Bagguley, D., Bash, K., Turner, V., Turnbull, S., Valtorta, N., & Caan, W. (2017). An overview of systematic reviews on the public health consequences of social isolation and loneliness. Public Health, 152, 157-171.
11. Matthews, T., Danese, A., Wertz, J., Odgers, C. L., Ambler, A., Moffitt, T. E., & Arseneault, L. (2019). Social isolation, loneliness and depression in young adulthood: A behavioural genetic analysis. Social Psychiatry and Psychiatric Epidemiology, 54(7), 877-887.
12. Rico-Uribe, L. A., Caballero, F. F., Martín-María, N., Cabello, M., Ayuso-Mateos, J. L., & Miret, M. (2018). Association of loneliness with all-cause mortality: A meta-analysis. PLoS One, 13(1), e0190033.
13. Shankar, A., Hamer, M., McMunn, A., & Steptoe, A. (2021). Social isolation and loneliness: Relationships with cognitive function during 4 years of follow-up in the English Longitudinal Study of Ageing. Psychological Medicine, 51(1), 75-83.

Further Reading:

1. Altman, B. (2013). The Startup Playbook: Secrets of the Fastest-Growing Startups from their Founding Entrepreneurs. Wiley.
2. Brown, B. (2012). Daring Greatly: How the Courage to Be Vulnerable Transforms the Way We Live, Love, Parent, and Lead. Avery.
3. Covey, S. R. (2013). The 7 Habits of Highly Effective People: Powerful Lessons in Personal Change. Simon & Schuster.
4. Duckworth, A. (2016). Grit: The Power of Passion and Perseverance. Scribner.
5. Dweck, C. S. (2006). Mindset: The New Psychology of Success. Ballantine Books.
6. Ferrazzi, K. (2014). Never Eat Alone: And Other Secrets to Success, One Relationship at a Time. Currency.

7. Ferriss, T. (2017). Tribe of Mentors: Short Life Advice from the Best in the World. Houghton Mifflin Harcourt.
8. Hoffman, R., & Casnocha, B. (2012). The Startup of You: Adapt to the Future, Invest in Yourself, and Transform Your Career. Crown Business.
9. Ismail, S., Malone, M. S., & van Geest, Y. (2014). Exponential Organisations: Why New Organisations Are Ten Times Better, Faster, and Cheaper Than Yours (and What to Do About It). Diversion Books.
10. Johnson, B. (2003). How to Talk to Anyone: 92 Little Tricks for Big Success in Relationships. McGraw-Hill Education.
11. Kawas, D. (2015). The Super Organizer: A Simple Guide to Getting Organized, Getting Productive and Getting Control of Your Life. Createspace Independent Pub.
12. Pink, D. H. (2011). Drive: The Surprising Truth About What Motivates Us. Riverhead Books.
13. Sinek, S. (2011). Start with Why: How Great Leaders Inspire Everyone to Take Action. Portfolio.
14. Sonnenfeldt, J. (2010). The Power of Failure: Succeeding in the Age of Innovation. Amacom.

Chapter 5: Balancing Work and Life

The Myth of Work-Life Balance and Its Impact on Mental Health

The concept of work-life balance has become a ubiquitous topic of discussion in modern society, often portrayed as an ideal state where individuals seamlessly manage their professional responsibilities alongside personal pursuits and family life. However, the pursuit of this balance can often feel like an elusive goal, leaving many individuals feeling overwhelmed and stressed. This chapter explores the myth of work-life balance, its impact on mental health, and strategies for effectively managing the demands of both work and personal life.

The concept of work-life balance implies a harmonious equilibrium between the time and energy allocated to work-related activities and those devoted to personal life, including family, leisure, and self-care. However, the reality is that achieving this equilibrium is often more complex than it seems. The rapid pace of technological advancement, globalisation, and the rise of remote working have blurred the boundaries between work and personal life, making it increasingly challenging for individuals to switch off from work-related responsibilities.

Research sheds light on the detrimental effects of blurred work-life boundaries on mental health. Gajendran and Harrison (2020) found that individuals who experienced high levels of work-life conflict reported increased symptoms of anxiety, depression, and burnout. Moreover, the prevalence of digital communication tools and the expectation of constant availability have further intensified these issues, leading to feelings of being constantly available and unable to fully disconnect from work and work-related stressors.

Clients have expressed increasing distress and anger towards employers particularly managers who blur and overstep boundaries repeatedly, thus leading to increased stress, disdain and eventually sickness absence or worse, presenteeism because they can see no way of addressing the issues without losing their jobs.

Presenteeism, the phenomenon where employees show up for work despite being unwell or otherwise unfit to perform optimally, poses significant challenges to both individuals and organisations. Presenteeism has gained increasing attention in organisational research due to its pervasive nature and adverse consequences. Unlike absenteeism, which involves employees being absent from work, presenteeism occurs when employees attend work despite illness, injury, or other health-related issues (Johns, 2010). Although presenteeism may seem like a display of dedication or commitment, it often reflects underlying issues such as job insecurity, excessive workload, or cultural norms that discourage taking time off (Aronsson, Gustafsson, & Dallner, 2000).

For entrepreneurs this is exacerbated further because they are solely responsible for the success or failure of their business. The pressure to create a successful business is great however it demands that the entrepreneur not only knows about their area of interest or expertise but that they are also accomplished and adept at everything else expected in entrepreneurship. For most new to the field, this is challenging and creates a steep learning curve that demands time and effort. Add to these, expectations of engaging in the responsibilities of everyday life, dealing with children, partners, pets, school runs, shopping, breakdowns (both mental and of household implements and cars), financial demands because the bills still need to be paid and very quickly, the cup flows over.

The pressure to achieve work-life balance can also perpetuate feelings of guilt and inadequacy, particularly among working parents who struggle to meet the demands of both their professional and family responsibilities.

Kossek et al. (2018) highlighted the challenges faced by working parents in managing competing priorities and the need for organisations to implement supportive policies and flexible work arrangements to alleviate the strain. Sadly, these adjustments are not available to entrepreneurs.

Causes, Impact, and Solutions for Anxiety, Stress, and Depression

Anxiety, stress, and depression are prevalent mental health challenges that can significantly impact an individual's overall well-being, including their personal health and relationships. Understanding the causes, effects, and effective remedies for these conditions is crucial for promoting mental wellness and achieving a healthier work-life balance.

Work-Related Pressures

High job demands, tight deadlines, and performance expectations can contribute to feelings of anxiety and stress. Grandey and Cropanzano (2016) found that job stressors such as workload, role ambiguity, and interpersonal conflict are associated with increased anxiety and psychological distress among employees. These and more pressures are present in entrepreneurial life as there is often little preset or prescribed order and structure to follow. For an entrepreneur, there is a steep learning curve including a great deal of trail and error to figure out how everything is supposed to work and which order is the most suitable and importantly, valuable in their particular area.

Work-Life Conflict

Difficulty balancing work and personal life responsibilities can exacerbate feelings of stress and depression. On one hand, the entrepreneur is often working hard to enhance their family's lifestyle, however, this comes at great cost as their success depends very much on their diligence and wholesale commitment to making their business work and do so successfully. Amstad et al. (2011) indicate that work-life conflict is a significant predictor of depressive symptoms, particularly among individuals with high work demands and limited resources for recovery. For an entrepreneur already working with limited resources, external demands add to the pressure and sense of overwhelm including feeling pulled in all directions.

Perfectionism

Striving for perfection in both professional and personal spheres can contribute to heightened anxiety and depression. Hewitt and Flett (2018) highlighted the detrimental effects of perfectionism on mental health, including increased levels of stress and depressive symptoms. It is important to bear in mind that perfectionism is rooted in fear of failure often informed by dysfunctional expectations or negative experiences of failure and criticism in the past leading to chronic stress, anxiety, dissatisfaction and decline in well-being in the present.

Setting realistic and manageable goals and practicing self-compassion during the entrepreneurial journey can have significant health benefits for those prone to perfectionistic tendencies. Therapy is another important tool to utilise to work through the underlying causes of perfectionism.

Impact on Personal Health and Relationships
Physical Health Consequences

As discussed in detail in Chapter 1, chronic stress and

anxiety can take a toll on physical health, leading to issues such as high blood pressure, cardiovascular disease, and weakened immune function. Cohen et al. (2016) demonstrated the link between chronic stress and increased susceptibility to infectious illnesses, highlighting the importance of managing stress for maintaining overall health.

Strained Relationships

Anxiety, stress, and depression can have a detrimental impact on relationships with family members, friends, and colleagues. Individuals experiencing these mental health pressures may withdraw socially, exhibit irritability or mood swings, and struggle to communicate effectively due to overwhelm. Whisman et al. (2016) found that depressive symptoms are associated with decreased relationship satisfaction and increased conflict within intimate partnerships. This is particularly prevalent in entrepreneurial relationships due to the amount of time invested in building a business and navigating the various steps required which impact on the time invested in personal relationships.

Impaired Cognitive Function

Brain fog and overwhelm caused by sustained anxiety and stress is known as impaired cognitive function. Impaired cognitive function can lead to difficulties with concentration, memory, and decision-making, qualities essential in setting up and running a business. Research by Lupien et al. (2018) demonstrated the negative impact of chronic stress on cognitive performance, highlighting the need for effective stress management strategies to preserve cognitive health. Despite feeling counter-intuitive especially for new entrepreneurs, taking time out to rest and recharge can significantly increase focus and productivity. Rest can increase the chances of gaining creative insights that can help resolve problems and help overcome hurdles.

Some Solutions for Addressing Stress and Anxiety
Cognitive-behavioural therapy (CBT)

CBT is a widely recognised and evidence-based treatment for anxiety, stress, and depression. This therapeutic approach focuses on identifying and challenging negative thought patterns and behaviours, teaching coping skills, and promoting relaxation techniques. Hofmann et al. (2012) have supported the efficacy of CBT in reducing symptoms of anxiety and depression across various populations. However, it is important to note that whilst CBT has been shown to produce positive results for *some* individuals, it is **not** a catch-all for everyone. Despite the adoption of CBT as a popular modality for therapy particularly used in trying to reduce waiting lists, it is not suitable for all presenting issues and should not be used as such.

Individuals who may be struggling with issues such as, but not limited to, bereavement, trauma or historical abuse or experiencing suicidal thoughts would benefit from different therapeutic modalities that are based on the Client-Centred approach of Humanistic Therapy which are less directive and prescriptive thus putting you, the client, at the centre of the supportive framework and enable you to work at your pace.

The Role of Psychotherapy in Self-Care Practice

Psychotherapy, also known as talk therapy and is a deeper broader form of counselling, as well as being a collaborative process between a trained therapist and an individual aimed at addressing psychological issues, improving emotional well-being, and promoting personal growth. In today's hectic world, where stress, anxiety, and burnout are increasingly prevalent, psychotherapy plays a crucial role in supporting individuals in their self-care journey.

What is Psychotherapy?

Counselling typically focuses on specific issues, challenges, or life transitions, such as relationship problems, career decisions, grief, stress management, or personal development. It often targets short-term goals and aims to help an individual identify and implement practical solutions, coping strategies, and support to help individuals overcome immediate difficulties. Counselling is typically a short-term arrangement.

Psychotherapy, on the other hand, tends to address deeper and more complex psychological issues, including long-standing patterns of behaviour, emotional struggles, mental health disorders, and unresolved traumas. It explores underlying thoughts, feelings and beliefs, aiming for deeper insight and lasting change and is typically a longer-term professional intervention.

Psychotherapy encompasses various therapeutic approaches, including Cognitive-Behavioural Therapy

(CBT), Psychodynamic Therapy, Humanistic Therapy, and Interpersonal Therapy, among others. The specific approach used depends on the individual's needs, preferences, and goals for therapy.

In psychotherapy, individuals have the opportunity to explore their thoughts, feelings, and behaviours in a safe and supportive environment. Through therapeutic interventions and evidence-based techniques, individuals gain insight into their inner experiences, develop coping strategies, and learn to navigate life's challenges more effectively.

The Importance of Psychotherapy in Self-Care

Research consistently demonstrates the efficacy of psychotherapy in promoting mental health and well-being. Cuijpers et al. (2016) found that psychotherapy is effective in treating a wide range of mental health conditions, including depression, anxiety disorders, and post-traumatic stress disorder (PTSD). Moreover, psychotherapy has been shown to improve overall functioning and quality of life.

In today's fast-paced and demanding work environments, psychotherapy offers a space for individuals to process stress, gain perspective on their experiences, and develop healthy coping mechanisms. By addressing underlying psychological issues and building emotional resilience, psychotherapy equips individuals with the tools they need to thrive in both their personal and professional lives.

Case Studies

Case Study 1: John's Journey to Work-Life Balance

John, a high-level executive in a tech company, was struggling to balance the expectations of his demanding job with his personal life. He often found himself working long hours, neglecting his health and relationships in the process. Despite his professional success, John felt increasingly stressed, anxious, and overwhelmed.

Recognising the need for support, John decided to seek psychotherapy. Through regular therapy sessions, John explored his work-related stressors, perfectionist tendencies, and underlying fears of failure. With the guidance of his therapist, John learned to set boundaries, prioritise self-care, and cultivate a healthier work-life balance.

Over time, John noticed significant improvements in his well-being and relationships. He became more present with his family, engaged in hobbies he enjoyed, and approached work with a greater sense of perspective and balance. Through psychotherapy, John not only prevented burnout but also rediscovered joy and fulfilment in both his professional and personal life.

Case Study 2: Sarah's Struggle with Burnout

Sarah, a successful entrepreneur running her own marketing agency, was on the verge of burnout. The pressure to meet tight deadlines, manage a team, and grow her business had taken a toll on her mental and physical health. Sarah found herself experiencing chronic stress, insomnia, and feelings of overwhelm.

Feeling overwhelmed and exhausted, Sarah turned to psychotherapy for support. In therapy, Sarah explored the underlying causes of her burnout, including perfectionism, imposter syndrome, and difficulty setting boundaries because her parents had repeatedly crossed any boundaries she had tried to assert during her childhood. With the help of her therapist, Sarah developed coping strategies to manage stress more effectively, challenge negative thought patterns, and prioritise self-care.

As Sarah committed to her therapeutic journey, she noticed significant improvements in her well-being and work performance. She learned to delegate tasks, set realistic goals and take regular breaks to recharge. Through psychotherapy, Sarah not only prevented burnout but also gained valuable insights into herself and her patterns of behaviour, empowering her to lead a more balanced and fulfilling life which included the ability to say 'no' more often.

Mindfulness Meditation

Mindfulness practices (also see **Ch. 3**), such as meditation and deep breathing exercises, have been shown to reduce stress, anxiety, and depressive symptoms. Mindfulness-based interventions can significantly help to improve emotional regulation and increase resilience to stress as documented by Keng et al. (2011). Furthermore, as a practice, when incorporated as a daily routine, it can have significant preventative properties toward the impact of stress related issues.

Social Support
Building and maintaining strong social support networks as discussed in the previous chapter can buffer against the negative effects of stress and depression particularly that caused by isolation as often experienced by entrepreneurs. Kawachi and Berkman's (2014) research found that social support is associated with improved mental health outcomes and greater resilience in the face of adversity. This is often connected with the dilutory impact of having someone to confide in and share concerns with. It is said that a problem shared is a problem halved. This can be true for meaningful connections that are supportive and nurturing.

Lifestyle Modifications
Adopting healthy lifestyle habits, such as regular exercise, balanced nutrition, adequate sleep and relaxation techniques, can support overall mental well-being. Research by Schuch et al. (2018) highlights the beneficial effects of physical activity on reducing symptoms of anxiety and depression, emphasising the importance of incorporating exercise into daily routines.

Anxiety, stress, and depression are multifaceted mental health challenges with far-reaching implications for personal health and relationships. By understanding the underlying causes, recognising the impact on well-being, and implementing effective remedies, individuals can proactively manage these conditions and cultivate a healthier work-life balance. Through evidence-based interventions such as cognitive-behavioural therapy, mindfulness meditation, social support, and lifestyle modifications, individuals can enhance their resilience, improve mental health outcomes and foster greater harmony between work and personal life.

Strategies for Setting Boundaries and Prioritising Self-Care
While achieving perfect work-life balance may be unrealistic and stressful in itself, there are strategies individuals can employ to establish healthier boundaries and prioritise self-care. One such strategy is setting clear boundaries between work and personal life. This may involve establishing designated work hours and creating physical or psychological barriers to delineate between workspaces and leisure spaces.

Brough et al. (2019) suggest that establishing these boundaries can help reduce work-life conflict and improve overall well-being. This is also imperative for entrepreneurs building their own business. Whilst the excitement of a new venture can be as exhilarating as falling in love, being unable to sleep or eat, leading to burning the midnight oil, negative habits can form and eventually cause problems.

Getting into a balanced routine early in the entrepreneurial journey can be beneficial in the long-term by reducing the impact of stressors and stress on the body and mind and keep the spirit buoyant for longer. A routine can also help ensure that other areas of your life are not neglected such as important and intimate relationships including the one with your Self.

Self-care is not a luxury; it's a necessity for maintaining optimal performance, especially for busy entrepreneurs. In the fast-paced world of business, the pressure to constantly perform, innovate, and excel can take a toll on both mental and physical health. Neglecting self-care not only jeopardises personal well-being but also undermines professional success in the long run.

Understanding the Importance of Self-Care for Sustainable Success

Research has shown that prioritising self-care leads to improved productivity, creativity, and resilience in the face of challenges. Sonnentag and Fritz (2015) found that engaging in regular self-care activities, such as exercise, mindfulness, and leisure pursuits, enhances well-being and reduces the risk of burnout among employees. They further emphasised the positive effects of engaging in leisure activities outside of work on reducing stress and replenishing cognitive resources. This includes engaging in activities that promote physical and mental well-being, such as exercise, meditation, hobbies and spending quality time with loved ones.

Similarly, Kuykendall, Tay, and Ng (2015) revealed a positive association between self-care practices and job performance across various industries. These findings can be applied to the entrepreneur equally.

Chapter 5: Balancing Work and Life

Self-care is not just about taking occasional breaks or pampering oneself; it involves adopting a holistic approach emphasised throughout this book, to well-being that encompasses physical, mental and emotional health. This means paying attention to diet, exercise, sleep, stress management, and interpersonal relationships. By investing in self-care and this includes elements such as professional coaching and therapy, entrepreneurs can replenish their energy reserves, sharpen their focus and sustain high levels of performance over the long term.

Effective Time Management

In addition to setting boundaries and prioritising self-care, effective time management is crucial for maintaining a sense of balance between work and personal life. This involves identifying priorities, setting realistic goals, and utilising tools and techniques to optimise productivity.

Francesco Cirillo developed the **Pomodoro Technique** in the 1980s, an effective time management approach to aid and enhance concentration and effectively completing goals, albeit in bite-sized pieces. This technique involves breaking work into segments, typically 25 minutes long, separated by short breaks.

Here's how it works:

1. Select a task or set of short tasks.
2. Pick one and do it with a timer for 25 minutes.
3. When the timer sounds take a 5 minute break.
4. Repeat as needed.

5. After 4 completed tasks, take a longer 15-30 minute break.

Cugelman et al's (2015) research suggests that the Pomodoro Technique can improve focus and productivity by harnessing the principles of timeboxing and frequent breaks. However, this may not be a long enough time period for some people who may struggle to concentrate and then break concentration; so try the above technique as guided and then increase the time until you find one that suits you. Creating a toolkit is about trialling things and finding what works for you.

Another useful time management tool is the **Eisenhower Matrix** which categorises tasks based on their urgency and importance. This helps individuals prioritise tasks and allocate their time and energy more effectively.

Here's How It Works:

1. A task that is important **and** urgent would be labelled as: **Do Now** on a matrix of 2x2 square grid
2. A task that is important **but not** urgent is labelled: **Schedule**
3. A task that is not important **but** urgent is labelled: **Delegate**
4. A task that is not important **and not** urgent is labelled: **Delete**

What current, pressing task can you use the Eisenhower Matrix with? Practicing with current or past issues will make you familiar with the concept and help you action it quickly when required.

	Urgent	Not Urgent
Important	Do Now	Schedule
Not Important	Delegate	Delete

Covey (2013) highlights the importance of distinguishing between urgent and important tasks to avoid getting caught up in busywork and focus on activities that align with long-term goals. Both techniques can be combined to streamline and speed up the work.

Summary

Achieving work-life balance is a multifaceted endeavour that requires conscious effort, self-awareness, and effective time management skills. While the concept of work-life balance may be idealised, the reality is that it is often more about finding harmony and integration between various aspects of life rather than striving for perfection. By setting boundaries, prioritising self-care, and managing time effectively, individuals can cultivate a healthier balance between work and personal life, leading to improved mental health and overall well-being.

Self Reflection Questions
1. Reflect on your current work-life balance. Are there areas where you feel you could improve? What steps could you take to achieve a greater sense of balance?
2. Consider the boundaries you have in place between work and personal life. How clear and effective are these boundaries? How could you strengthen them?
3. Think about your current time management strategies. Are there techniques or tools you could incorporate to enhance your productivity and efficiency?
4. Reflect on the concept of self-care. What activities bring you joy and replenish your energy? How can you prioritise these activities in your daily life?
5. Consider your long-term goals and priorities. Are the tasks and activities you engage in aligned with these goals? If not, what adjustments could you make to better align your actions with your aspirations?

Bibliography:
1. Amstad, F. T., Meier, L. L., Fasel, U., Elfering, A., & Semmer, N. K. (2011). A meta-analysis of work–family conflict and various outcomes with a special emphasis on cross-domain versus matching-domain relations. Journal of Occupational Health Psychology, 16(2), 151–169.
2. Aronsson, G., Gustafsson, K., & Dallner, M. (2000). Sick but yet at work. An empirical study of sickness presenteeism. Journal of Epidemiology and Community Health, 54(7), 502–509.
3. Brough, P., O'Driscoll, M. P., & Kalliath, T. (2019). Work-family enrichment, conflict, and family-supportive organisation perceptions: A cross-national analysis. Journal of Managerial Psychology, 34(5), 317–332.

Chapter 5: Balancing Work and Life

4. Cohen, S., Janicki-Deverts, D., & Miller, G. E. (2016). Psychological stress and disease. JAMA, 298(14), 1685–1687.
5. Covey, S. R. (2013). The 7 habits of highly effective people: Powerful lessons in personal change. Simon and Schuster.
6. Cugelman, B., Thelwall, M., & Dawes, P. (2015). Online interventions for social marketing health behaviour change campaigns: A meta-analysis of psychological architectures and adherence factors. Journal of Medical Internet Research, 17(1), e17.
7. Gajendran, R. S., & Harrison, D. A. (2020). Work–family conflict and employee well-being: A meta-analysis. Journal of Applied Psychology, 105(2), 147–192.
8. Grandey, A. A., & Cropanzano, R. (2016). The conservation of resources model applied to work–family conflict and strain. Journal of Vocational Behaviour, 98, 30–44.
9. Hewitt, P. L., & Flett, G. L. (2018). Perfectionism and depression: A multidimensional analysis. Journal of Social and Clinical Psychology, 37(8), 678–695.
10. Hofmann, S. G., Asnaani, A., Vonk, I. J., Sawyer, A. T., & Fang, A. (2012). The efficacy of cognitive behavioural therapy: A review of meta-analyses. Cognitive Therapy and Research, 36(5), 427–440.
11. Johns, G. (2010). Presenteeism in the workplace: A review and research agenda. Journal of Organisational Behaviour, 31(4), 519–542.
12. Kawachi, I., & Berkman, L. F. (2014). Social capital, social cohesion, and health. In Social Epidemiology (pp. 290–319). Oxford University Press.
13. Keng, S. L., Smoski, M. J., & Robins, C. J. (2011). Effects of mindfulness on psychological health: A review of empirical studies. Clinical Psychology Review, 31(6), 1041–1056.
14. Kossek, E. E., Lautsch, B. A., & Eaton, S. C. (2018). Telecommuting, control, and boundary management: Correlates of policy use and practice, job control, and work–family effectiveness. Journal of Vocational Behaviour, 107, 128–142.
15. Lupien, S. J., McEwen, B. S., Gunnar, M. R., & Heim, C. (2018). Effects of stress throughout the lifespan on the brain, behaviour and cognition. Nature Reviews Neuroscience, 10(6), 434–445.
16. Pennebaker, J. W. (1997). Opening up: The healing power of expressing emotions. Guilford Press.
17. Pennebaker, J. W., & Beall, S. K. (1986). Confronting a traumatic event: Toward an understanding of inhibition and disease. Journal of Abnormal Psychology, 95(3), 274–281.
18. Schuch, F. B., Vancampfort, D., Firth, J., Rosenbaum, S., Ward, P. B., Silva, E. S., ... & Stubbs, B. (2018). Physical activity and incident depression: A meta-analysis of prospective cohort studies. American Journal of Psychiatry, 175(7), 631–648.

19. Sonnentag, S., & Fritz, C. (2015). Recovery from job stress: The stressor-detachment model as an integrative framework. Journal of Organisational Behaviour, 36(S1), S72–S103.
20. Whisman, M. A., Beach, S. R., & Snyder, D. K. (2016). Is marital discord taxonic and can taxonic status be assessed reliably? Results from a national, representative sample of married couples. Journal of Consulting and Clinical Psychology, 84(12), 1121–1135.

Further Reading:

1. Brown, B. (2010). The gifts of imperfection: Let go of who you think you're supposed to be and embrace who you are. Hazelden Publishing.
2. Clear, J. (2018). Atomic habits: An easy & proven way to build good habits & break bad ones. Avery.
3. Dweck, C. S. (2007). Mindset: The new psychology of success. Random House.
4. Gazipura, A. (2017). Not nice: Stop people pleasing, staying silent, & feeling guilty... and start speaking up, saying no, asking boldly, and unapologetically being yourself. Life Mastery Institute.
5. Manson, M. (2016). The subtle art of not giving a f*ck: A counterintuitive approach to living a good life. HarperOne.
6. McDonagh, B. (2015). Dare: The new way to end anxiety and stop panic attacks fast. BMD Publishing.
7. Nagoski, E., & Nagoski, A. (2019). Burnout: The secret to unlocking the stress cycle. Ballantine Books.
8. Newport, C. (2016). Deep work: Rules for focused success in a distracted world. Grand Central Publishing.
9. Tolle, E. (2004). The power of now: A guide to spiritual enlightenment. New World Library.
10. Achor, S. (2010). The happiness advantage: How a positive brain fuels success in work and life. Crown Business.

Chapter 6: Overcoming Imposter Syndrome

Understanding Imposter Syndrome and its Prevalence Among Entrepreneurs

Imposter syndrome is a psychological mindset in which individuals doubt their accomplishments and have a persistent fear of being exposed as a fraud, despite evidence of their competence or success. This phenomenon is prevalent among entrepreneurs due to the high levels of risk, uncertainty and responsibility inherent in entrepreneurship. In this chapter, we will explore the nature of imposter syndrome, its impact on entrepreneurs, and strategies for overcoming it.

Imposter syndrome was first identified in the 1970s by psychologists Pauline Clance and Suzanne Imes they found that it affects people across various fields, including business and entrepreneurship. Chrisman et al., (2020) found that imposter syndrome is particularly common among entrepreneurs, with approximately 58% reporting experiencing it at some point in their careers.

Entrepreneurs are especially susceptible to imposter syndrome due to the nature of their work. The entrepreneurial journey is fraught with challenges, including financial instability, intense competition and the pressure to innovate and succeed. These factors can exacerbate feelings of self-doubt and inadequacy, leading entrepreneurs to question their abilities and accomplishments.

Imposter syndrome doesn't just affect entrepreneurs, it is prevalent in almost every area of life. From highly accomplished global leaders such as Michelle Obama, to motivational speakers like Mel Robbins and the immeasurable **Dr Maya Angelou** who spoke about her constant fear of being found out:

> "I have written eleven books, but each time I think, 'Uh oh, they're going to find out now. I've run a game on everybody, and they're going to find me out.'"

This quote encapsulates the essence of imposter syndrome, the persistent fear of being exposed as a fraud despite evidence of success. This phenomenon isn't just relegated to people in the public eye. Supremely accomplished leaders such as **Indra Nooyi**, the former CEO of PepsiCo, has spoken about her experiences with imposter syndrome.

> "Imposter syndrome is something I struggled with. I still do, every now and then. You think, 'Why would anyone want to listen to me? I don't have anything important to say.'"

Nooyi's candid acknowledgment reflects the pervasive nature of imposter syndrome, even among highly accomplished individuals. So it is no surprise that Jane

Chapter 6: Overcoming Imposter Syndrome

Public about to start on her entrepreneurial journey may feel anxiety and trepidation.

Dr Valerie Young (2011) has identified and highlighted five types of Imposter Syndrome through her research with high achieving, successful women reporting feeling like a fraud. She found that Imposter Syndrome appeared as five sub-groups in her sample and included: the Perfectionist, the Superwoman/man, the Natural Genius, the Soloist and the Expert. These are referred to as competence types. Let's look at a couple of these.

The Perfectionist is a frequent and uninvited guest in my client's lives. Let's take Jane, a highly qualified and accomplished Consultant in the medical profession and at the top of her field, highly regarded and respected by colleagues. On the face of it, Jane should be celebrating her accomplishments and the regard in which she is held, but she isn't. Crippling self doubt rooted in a difficult and hyper-critical childhood have affected her ability to trust in herself and others. Jane came to therapy with burnout. Her third. She had been signed off after finally reaching out for help, something that exacerbated her need for perfectionism, feelings of Imposter Syndrome, guilt, anxiety, anger, frustration, sadness and exasperation.

Whilst reticent at first, Jane slowly engaged with the therapy and opened up about the toxic environment in which she was raised with her siblings. Her father was absent, preferring to stay out of the house whenever possible and her mother was extremely critical. Nothing

Jane or her siblings did was good enough. They were criticised and put down about everything by their mother. This planted the seed of trying to be the best at whatever she tried if only to stop her mother's shrill voice.

Now, in her late 30's, single and signed off, Jane shared that she struggled to trust people and had never allowed herself to rely on anyone, after all, why should she, when she had been repeatedly let down and each time it had taken a great deal of time to heal from the disappointment? At work this translated to being Superwoman, refusing to delegate work despite having a team of staff that she was responsible for and whose job it was to do some of the tasks she took on herself. This meant that she was constantly stretched and exhausted which impacted her personal life and ability for close relationships and have support.

Over the course of therapy, Jane slowly learned that not only did she have a strong perfectionistic driver, but she ticked off the other categories proposed by Young as well. However, Jane also learned to reclaim and champion that hurting Inner Child through our work and rewrite the scripts she had internalised from her critical mother.

Imposter Syndrome despite being prevalent, isn't a life-sentence. With the right support and techniques, it can be challenged and replaced with more self-caring behaviours which are essential in business and life.

Chapter 6: Overcoming Imposter Syndrome

Techniques for Combating Self-Doubt and Embracing Success

Whilst imposter syndrome can be debilitating, there are several techniques that entrepreneurs can employ to combat it and build confidence in their abilities:

Recognise and Acknowledge Feelings of Self-Doubt

The first step in overcoming imposter syndrome is to acknowledge and accept the presence of these feelings. By recognising that self-doubt is a common experience shared by many entrepreneurs, individuals can begin to challenge the negative beliefs that contribute to imposter syndrome. An important truth is that some amount of fear and trepidation necessary in any venture because it prevents arrogance and over-confidence which can lead to failure.

Use journalling to write down fears and concerns, ask yourself, 'what's the worst that can happen if I delegate?' for example. In Jane's case she was fearful of the project not getting done and if it was, it wouldn't be to *her* standards therefore her automatic response was to do it herself thus increasing her own workload and pressure to achieve unreasonably high standards that had led to multiple experiences of burnout. The core element that drove her behaviour was rooted in fear of ridicule, rejection and shaming from authority figures, no different to that she had experienced throughout her childhood. For Jane, learning and acknowledging that she was now an authority figure in her own right and was more than capable of identifying if something wasn't up to standard helped her slowly trust herself and others.

Use the Eisenhower Matrix in the previous chapter to help you prioritise work. If you are able, delegate some tasks, start with small ones and work up to more important ones.

Challenge Negative Thoughts

Entrepreneurship often involves taking risks and stepping outside of one's comfort zone, which can trigger feelings of inadequacy. When faced with negative thoughts or self-critical beliefs, entrepreneurs can challenge them by examining the evidence supporting these beliefs and reframing them in a more positive light. For example, instead of thinking 'I'm not qualified to run my own business,' entrepreneurs can remind themselves of their relevant skills, experiences, and achievements that demonstrate their capability. One powerful technique is to update your CV or resume.

Yousuf approached me to help him cope with crippling bouts of anxiety and catastrophic thinking. He was accomplished in the financial sector with multiple awards and plaudits from his peers and had wanted to set up his own business since he was a teen. However, he had been pressured to go into employment by concerned parents who had lost a large amount of money in a failed business venture that had decimated their life savings and almost caused them to lose their house.

We explored the root cause of the anxiety – his parents' expectations of him and his own desire to grow in his own right. Yousouf had done the research, knew that his niche was stable and reliable with average competition and he'd built up the experience on the job so knew to look out for the pitfalls, something his parents hadn't had the luxury to do.

I also invited Yousouf to update his cv and explained that he needed to see in black and white what he had achieved and was capable of. This was a game-changer for Yousouf's mindset because there, in a simple exercise and document, he could see his professional journey and progression as well as the staggering amount of experience and skillset he had accumulated.

Stepping back from the issue and looking at the facts helped Yousouf to reduce the crippling anxiety and be able to reassure his parents that he was more than able to set up his own consultancy and make it successful.

Seek Support and Feedback
Building a strong support network of mentors, peers, and advisors can help entrepreneurs navigate the challenges of entrepreneurship and provide valuable feedback and encouragement. By seeking support from others who have experienced similar struggles, entrepreneurs can gain perspective and reassurance that they are not alone in their feelings of self-doubt.

Having even one trusted and valued individual offering support can have a significant a positive impact for an entrepreneur. Explore your current personal and professional network, who stands out as someone you trust and can reach out to for support? Consider the type of support you specifically need and whether this person has the capacity to offer it?

For some support may look like practical help; please can you read this for me? Please will you come to a networking meeting with me?

For some it may be emotional support; please will you sit and speak with me about this issue?

For others still, it may simply be the knowledge that there is someone out there that they can call IF they need to – like insurance, a reassurance that it is in place if needed.

The important thing is to be proactive in identifying what kind of support you need and finding the courage to ask.

Set Realistic Goals and Celebrate Successes

Setting achievable goals and celebrating milestones along the entrepreneurial journey can help boost confidence and motivation. By breaking down larger objectives into smaller, manageable tasks, entrepreneurs can track their progress and acknowledge their accomplishments along the way.

Remember the Pomodoro Technique in the last chapter? Using this with projects can help accomplish tasks and offer a great deal of reassurance and offer a cause for celebration. There are those that balk at the idea of celebrating small wins, however, doing so not only reinforces the most recent accomplishment but offers motivation to repeat the thing that created the good-feeling within.

Affirmation Exercises and Reframing Techniques

Affirmation exercises and reframing techniques are powerful tools for overcoming imposter syndrome and cultivating a positive mindset. These techniques involve consciously challenging negative beliefs and replacing them with affirmations or positive scripts used with ourselves.

Affirmation Exercises

Affirmations are positive statements that affirm one's worth, abilities, and potential for success. Affirmations have been present throughout history in the form of chants and mantras that highlight and celebrate the multiple positive attributes of divine entities. In Hinduism the self is seen as a representation of divinity and therefore imbibed with the attributes and power inherent in the Divine.

Unfortunately, this has been forgotten and there is a distinct detachment from divine virtues. Through experiences of criticism and judgement, many use critical self-talk leading to self-loathing and result in mental health issues.

Louise Hay, a metaphysical teacher found that critical thoughts and scripts were linked to dis-ease and physical illness in the body. Her immense body of work has helped millions of people reframe their critical thinking through the use of affirmations, self-love and self-acceptance practices.

Affirmations are positive scripts used to challenge and replace negative and toxic thought patterns that lead to low self-esteem and poor self-regard. Hay's positive statements are aimed at reprogramming the subconscious mind to cultivate self-love, self-acceptance, and healing. She believed that by repeating affirmations regularly, individuals could overcome negative thought patterns and manifest positive changes in their lives.

Hay's Affirmations Include:
1. I am safe, and all is well.
2. I love and approve of my Self
3. I am surrounded by love wherever I go
4. Only good shall come out of this situation.
5. I am deserving of love, kindness, and respect.
6. I am worthy of all the good things life has to offer.
7. I forgive myself and release all feelings of guilt and shame.
8. I trust in the process of life and know that everything happens for my highest good.
9. I am capable, confident, and courageous in all that I do.
10. I love and accept myself exactly as I am.
11. I am surrounded by abundance, and I attract prosperity into my life.
12. I choose to let go of fear and embrace the limitless possibilities of the universe.
13. I am grateful for the blessings in my life and I attract more blessings every day.
14. I am a magnet for love, happiness, and success.
15. I am capable of overcoming any challenge.
16. I deserve to succeed in my ventures.

Chapter 6: Overcoming Imposter Syndrome

These affirmations are designed to foster self-love, empowerment, and positivity. Feel free to use them regularly to support your well-being and personal growth. If the above don't resonate, 'I am enough' is incredibly powerful to start resetting a critical inner voice.

Hay also believed that physical ailments are often connected to unresolved emotional issues or negative beliefs. Through her work on the mind-body connection Hay advocated for the use of affirmations, visualizations, and forgiveness practices as tools for healing both the body and the mind believing that the release of toxic thinking would free the body to heal and be restored to vibrancy.

Self-love was also an important aspect of self-acceptance for Hay who believed that learning to love ourselves was essential to living a peaceful life that encouraged personal growth and well-being. This is particularly important for entrepreneurs because of the weight of their tasks and the doubts that arise about their capacity or whether their business will succeed or not. After all, how can you champion yourself or your business if you dislikes or hate yourself?

By repeating affirmations regularly, entrepreneurs can reprogram their subconscious mind and reinforce positive beliefs about themselves.

Reframing Techniques
Reframing involves changing the way one perceives a situation or thought by looking at it from a different perspective. This is an essential skill to master. The

entrepreneur's world can be chaotic and difficult more often than not in the beginning. There are multiple things to address, review, juggle and deal with. If one thing goes wrong, it may not feel like the end of the world, however, when multiple things are going wrong, the pressure can be overwhelming.

Reframing a situation can have a significant impact on the ability to cope with what is going on. It is easy to catastrophise things when overwhelmed however, being able to step back from the situation and look at it objectively can be empowering and reassuring.

For example, a business owner may be overwhelmed by someone opening an identical business next door. There are a multitude of feelings and emotions that can arise including a great deal of fear from expected competition and loss of business not to mention hostility. This is understandable, as it can be a challenging situation to navigate. However, it's important to recognise that hostility typically doesn't serve anyone well in the long run.

Reframing the situation can help the business owner manage their emotions and find constructive ways to address the challenges they face. Here's how they could approach it:

Original perspective: 'I feel hostile towards the new identical business next door because I see them as a threat to my business.'

Chapter 6: Overcoming Imposter Syndrome

Reframed perspective: 'The presence of the new identical business next door is an opportunity for me to reassess and strengthen my own business strategies.'

From this reframed perspective, the business owner can consider the following:

1. **Self-assessment**: Rather than focusing on the new competition, the business owner can use this opportunity to assess their own business strengths and weaknesses objectively. They can identify areas for improvement, such as customer service, marketing, or product offerings, and take proactive steps to address them.

2. **Adaptation**: The presence of competition can be a catalyst for innovation and adaptation. The business owner can use the situation as motivation to explore new ideas, improve their offerings, or find creative ways to attract and retain customers.

3. **Market differentiation**: Instead of viewing the new business as a direct threat, the business owner can focus on what sets their business apart. They can emphasise their unique selling points, such as exceptional quality, expertise in their field, personalised service, or exclusive products, to differentiate themselves in the market.

4. **Community engagement**: Building positive relationships with customers and the local community can help the business owner strengthen their position in the market. They can focus on providing value, building trust, and fostering loyalty among their existing customer base.

By reframing the situation and focusing on constructive actions, the business owner can channel their energy into strategies that will ultimately benefit their business in the long term, rather than being consumed by hostility towards the new competition.

When faced with self-doubt or negative thoughts, entrepreneurs can reframe them by focusing on their strengths, past successes, and lessons learned from failures. For example, instead of viewing failure as evidence of incompetence, entrepreneurs can reframe it as an opportunity for growth and learning.

Summary

In this chapter, we explored the nature of imposter syndrome, its prevalence among entrepreneurs, and strategies for overcoming it. Imposter syndrome is a common experience among entrepreneurs, stemming from the high levels of risk, uncertainty and responsibility inherent in entrepreneurship but also informed by the original often critical and dismissive programming of mindset in childhood by primary caregivers or important figures such as teachers.

To combat imposter syndrome, entrepreneurs can employ techniques such as recognising and challenging negative thoughts, seeking support and feedback, setting realistic goals, and celebrating successes. Additionally, affirmation exercises and reframing techniques can help entrepreneurs cultivate a positive mindset and build confidence in their abilities.

Chapter 6: Overcoming Imposter Syndrome

Self Reflection Questions:
1. Have you ever experienced feelings of self-doubt or imposter syndrome in your entrepreneurial journey? If so, how did you cope with these feelings?
2. What are some negative beliefs or thoughts that contribute to your imposter syndrome? How can you challenge and reframe these beliefs in a more positive light?
3. Identify three affirmations that resonate with you and reflect your strengths, abilities, and potential for success. How can you incorporate these affirmations into your daily routine?

References:

Chrisman, J. J., Bauerschmidt, A., Hofer, C. W., & Kay, E. (2020). The impact of entrepreneur's imposter syndrome on the strategic behaviours and outcomes of new firms. International Journal of Entrepreneurial Behaviour & Research, 26(8), 1949-1973.

Further Reading:

1. Brown, B. (2010). The gifts of imperfection: Let go of who you think you're supposed to be and embrace who you are.
2. Brown, B. (2012). Daring greatly: How the courage to be vulnerable transforms the way we live, love, parent, and lead.
3. Brown, B. (2015). Rising strong: How the ability to reset transforms the way we live, love, parent, and lead.
4. Brown, B. (2017). Braving the wilderness: The quest for true belonging and the courage to stand alone.
5. Dweck, C. S. (2007). Mindset: The new psychology of success.
6. Maté, G. (2003). In the realm of hungry ghosts: Close encounters with addiction.
7. Maté, G. (2003). When the body says no: The cost of hidden stress.
8. Oprah Winfrey. (2014). What I know for sure.
9. Oprah Winfrey. (2017). The wisdom of Sundays: Life-changing insights from super soul conversations.
10. Oprah Winfrey. (2019). The path made clear: Discovering your life's direction and purpose.

11. Ruiz, D. M. (1997). The four agreements: A practical guide to personal freedom.
12. Sincero, J. (2013). You are a badass: How to stop doubting your greatness and start living an awesome life.

Chapter 7: The Power of Positive Thinking

Exploring the Science of Positivity and Its Effects on Performance

Positive thinking, often championed as a remedy for life's challenges, holds a profound influence on our mental and physical well-being. Its effects ripple through our lives, shaping our perceptions, decisions and ultimately, our intentions and life choices. In this chapter, we delve into the science behind positivity and its remarkable impacts on performance.

The Neuroscience of Positivity

Neuroscientific research has unveiled the intricate mechanisms underlying positive thinking. Studies employing neuroimaging techniques, such as functional magnetic resonance imaging (fMRI), have illuminated the neural circuits involved in processing positive emotions. Key brain regions concerned include the prefrontal cortex, associated with decision-making and emotional regulation, and the amygdala, involved in emotion processing and the stress response.

Recent studies have highlighted the important role of

neurotransmitters such as dopamine and serotonin in modulating mood and reinforcing positive outlooks. For instance, Brown et al (2022) demonstrated how dopamine release in response to positive stimuli facilitates learning and motivation, promoting adaptive behaviours. Positive stimuli include being acknowledged and celebrated, remember the gold star at school, or the hearty well-done from someone important encouraging you to WANT to do better and achieve more?

Positive Thinking and Performance
The relationship between positive thinking and performance is multifaceted. Numerous studies have underscored the beneficial effects of a positive mindset across diverse domains, including academic achievement, athletic performance and professional success.

Fredrickson (2009) showed that cultivating positive emotions broadens individuals' cognitive repertoires, enhancing creativity and problem-solving abilities. Thus, a happier person is more relaxed and therefore open to explore different approaches to dealing with a problem compared to someone stressed and struggling to maintain any level of positivity.

Research on attitudes and performance by Luthans and Youssef (2007) demonstrated that employees with positive attitudes are not only more productive but also exhibit higher levels of job satisfaction and organisational commitment. This is further enhanced by positive leadership styles which have been shown to foster a supportive work environment, nurturing employee well-being and fostering innovation.

It is important to mention Toxic Positivity here. Whilst genuine positivity has significant benefits to mental health and well-being, toxic positivity does the opposite. Toxic positivity refers to the overemphasis on positive thinking to the extent that it dismisses or invalidates *valid* negative emotions or experiences. It often involves the pressure to maintain a relentlessly positive attitude often as a fear-based response to avoiding shame at any cost, even in the face of adversity or genuine struggles.

Therefore, while positivity can be beneficial, toxic positivity can have negative consequences, such as ignoring or suppressing important emotions, invalidating others' experiences, and failing to address underlying issues. It's important to acknowledge and validate all emotions, both positive and negative, in a healthy and balanced way.

Techniques for Cultivating a Positive Mindset

Cultivating a positive mindset is akin to tending a garden – it requires deliberate effort and consistent practice. Fortunately, an array of evidence-based techniques exist to nurture positivity and harness its transformative power.

Gratitude Practices

Gratitude, the practice of acknowledging and appreciating the good in one's life, serves as a cornerstone of positive psychology. Emmons and McCullough (2003) demonstrated that regularly expressing gratitude not only enhances subjective well-being but also promotes physical health and strengthens social relationships. Offering gratitude to another in acknowledgement of their impact plays a significant role in strengthening the bond within the relationship and foster a sense of connection and belonging.

Practicing gratitude increases emotional stability and a feeling of well-being offering a sense of safety and calmness in a sometimes-overwhelming world. Additional benefits include better sleep, increased resilience and a balanced view of the world particularly countering the detrimental impact of exposure to constant news cycles of war and tragedy.

Practical exercises, such as keeping a gratitude journal or writing thank-you notes, can foster a habit of gratitude and amplify its benefits by encouraging the mind to purposely and meaningful focus on the positives present.

Jaxon, a client struggling with not being able to switch off, reported a significant shift when he started a gratitude journal. Being averse to writing and to doing the exercise because he had no faith in its efficacy, he started with saying things he was grateful for out loud. He then progressed to writing single words on post-it notes.

After a couple of weeks, he noticed a slight difference in his mood and anxiety levels stating that it made him 'realise that it wasn't all one hundred percent bad'. After a month he decided to try writing down three gratitude statements and found that these helped him so much that he kept a small notebook with him to document things he felt grateful for throughout the day. As a result of the success he experienced, Jaxon was exploring the idea of journalling to help him document and process the issues that had affected him.

By consciously focusing on blessings or positive attributes, individuals can reframe their perspectives, foster resilience, enhance well-being and emotional equilibrium whilst also putting negative experiences in perspective.

Cognitive Restructuring
Cognitive restructuring involves challenging and reframing negative thought patterns to promote a more positive outlook. Drawing from Cognitive-Behavioural Therapy (CBT), this technique empowers individuals to identify distorted thinking styles, such as catastrophising or personalisation, and replace them with more balanced interpretations.

Take our shocked business owner facing competition earlier in chapter 6. The initial realisation of the threat to their livelihood by a competitor felt catastrophic because they had worked incredibly hard to set up their business. However, restructuring helped them realise that they not only had choices, but that they could take action to address the problem meaningfully and supercharge their business, mindset and future growth.

Beck et al (2015) highlighted the efficacy of cognitive restructuring in alleviating symptoms of depression and anxiety. By cultivating cognitive flexibility as a regular practice and promoting adaptive coping strategies, individuals can navigate adversity with greater ease and resilience.

Positive Affirmations
Positive affirmations as discussed in the previous chapter entail the repetition of empowering statements to instil confidence and self-belief. Although Hay's work was initially met with scepticism, research by Wood and Perunovic (2009) demonstrated that affirmations can bolster self-esteem and enhance performance in challenging tasks.

Effective affirmations are specific, believable, and aligned with one's values and goals. By internalising positive self-talk, individuals can counteract self-doubt, actively challenge negative self-talk and cultivate a resilient mindset grounded in self-efficacy. Research in neuroplasticity has offered evidence that learning and growth continues to occur across the lifespan thus, old patterns *can* be broken and new ones created. It appears that you *can* teach an old dog new tricks after all.

Strategies for Overcoming Negativity Bias
Despite the profound benefits of positivity, humans are evolutionarily predisposed towards negativity bias – a tendency to dwell on threats and setbacks while emphasising negative experiences and overlooking positive ones. This bias likely evolved as a survival mechanism, where being hyper-aware and hyper-vigilant towards potential threats helped our ancestors like Dave

and his chums avoid danger. In ancestral environments, being attuned to threats like predators, enemy tribes or scarce resources was crucial for survival. Those who were more vigilant and ready to respond to potential dangers were more likely to survive and pass on their genes.

These experiences are encoded genetically and present in the brain's amygdala which is responsible for processing emotions and tends to react more strongly to negative stimuli than positive ones because of conditioning over millennia. This heightened sensitivity to negativity influences our thoughts, emotions and behaviour in the present. Whilst we may no longer need to worry about physical threat and danger from wild animals, we are nonetheless exposed to threats that have the same impact on our emotional and physical being on a daily basis in our lives from stress as discussed in chapter 1.

Naturally, prolonged exposure from threats, especially those that can't be seen or prepared for, can lead to hypervigilance, pessimism, rumination, anxiety and depression. It can also affect self-confidence, decision-making, interpersonal relationships and overall well-being leading to withdrawal and isolation. Whilst stepping back can be beneficial and allow objectivity, it can also be detrimental if prolonged and lead to avoidant behaviours including not wanting to be at work or presenteeism, being at work but not being productive. Overcoming this inherent bias requires conscious effort and strategic interventions including being mindful about preventing slipping into old routines and belief systems.

Negativity creates immense stress in the body as discussed in chapter 1 and can have significant impact on the body, both in the short term and over time. Some of these impacts include, but are not limited to:

Stress Response
Negative emotions like anxiety, fear, or anger trigger the body's stress response, releasing stress hormones like cortisol and adrenaline. Chronic activation of the stress response can lead to elevated blood pressure, increased heart rate, and weakened immune function.

Immune System Suppression
Prolonged stress and negative emotions can suppress the immune system, making individuals more susceptible to infections, illnesses and autoimmune disorders such as lupus and fibromyalgia. Chronic inflammation, linked to negative emotions, is also associated with a range of health problems, including diabetes, and cancer.

Cardiovascular Health
Negativity and chronic stress contribute to the development and progression of cardiovascular diseases like hypertension, heart disease, and stroke. Elevated stress hormones and increased blood pressure put strain on the heart and blood vessels, raising the risk of heart attacks and other cardiac events.

Sleep Disturbances
Negative emotions and stress can disrupt sleep patterns, leading to difficulty falling asleep, frequent awakenings, and poor sleep quality. Inadequate sleep not only

Chapter 7: The Power of Positive Thinking

exacerbates negative emotions but also impairs cognitive function, mood regulation, and overall well-being adding increased pressure in trying to achieve day to day tasks.

Digestive Problems
Stress and negativity can affect the digestive system, leading to symptoms like stomach pain, acid reflux, bloating, and irritable bowel syndrome (IBS). Chronic stress may also alter gut microbiota composition, which can impact digestion and nutrient absorption.

Musculoskeletal Issues
Negative emotions often manifest physically as muscle tension, headaches, and body aches. Consider the concept of having a 'weight' on your head or shoulders as a metaphor for feeing emotionally weighed down, it makes sense, then that this will exert a physical load on the body. Chronic stress can contribute to the development of musculoskeletal disorders like body pain, tension headaches and other chronic pain conditions.

Mental Health Disorders
Prolonged exposure to negativity and stress increases the risk of developing mental health disorders such as depression, anxiety, and post-traumatic stress disorder (PTSD). These conditions not only affect mood and behaviour but also have profound effects on physical health and functioning. Overwhelm from constant worry impacts the ability to fully function emotionally thus adding to the stress already present. This self-

perpetuating cycle can lead to burnout, feelings of desperation and suicidal tendencies. Engaging in therapy can help alleviate the stress and help you learn techniques to strengthen self-care practices and build resilience.

The mind-body connection is powerful and negative emotions can significantly impact physical health and well-being. Addressing negativity through various therapeutic techniques including getting the root cause, stress management strategies and lifestyle interventions can help mitigate these effects and promote overall health and resilience.

Being positive and upbeat all the time is not natural, can be difficult and an unattainable and unreasonable expectation in a world that is stressful and sometimes challenging particularly as an entrepreneur. Exercises throughout this book if utilised, will significantly help to lessen the impact of stress and feelings that can lead to negativity.

Reframing Failure as Feedback

To this end let's acknowledge the presence of failure as part of the entrepreneurial journey. Failure is an inevitable aspect of the human experience, yet its interpretation, informed by past experiences and mind maps profoundly shapes individuals' responses and future trajectories (see **Chapter 9**).

Responding strongly to failure is to be human, some people may feel eviscerated because of their beliefs and conditioning around the concept. In many cultures failure carries incredible shame and its impact varies across cultures influencing behaviour, emotions and social interactions as well as impacting a personal sense of safety and well-being.

In some cultures, shame serves as a powerful tool for social control and conformity, while in others, it can lead to individual distress and withdrawal. For instance, in collectivist cultures like Japan, shame often regulates behaviour to maintain harmony and honour (Lebra, 1976). Conversely, in individualistic cultures such as the United States, shame may be associated with personal failure and stigma (Tangney & Dearing, 2002). Overall, cultural norms and values shape the experience and expression of shame, impacting psychological well-being and social dynamics including the negative impact of seeking professional help and support.

How an individual views failure is as important as its impact on their mental health and well-being. Seeing it as a catastrophic event can cause distress, disconnection and isolation in individuals raised through shaming and ridicule. However, for those who had supportive and encouraging environments and experiences, failure presents an opportunity to reassess what went wrong, why and how to address it until it works.

But what about those that didn't have a great experience? Therapy with a seasoned and experienced therapist will help individuals reframe their experiences and learn how to challenge negative self-talk and move forward with self-compassion and kindness.

Dweck (2006) highlighted the importance of adopting a growth mindset – the belief that abilities can be developed through dedication and effort. By viewing challenges as opportunities for growth, individuals can transcend fear of failure and pursue their aspirations with renewed vigour. By reframing failure as an opportunity for learning rather than a reflection of inadequacy, individuals can extract valuable insights and grow from setbacks.

Practising Self-Compassion

Self-compassion, the practice of extending kindness and understanding towards oneself in times of struggle, serves as a powerful antidote to negativity bias. Neff's (2003) research has repeatedly demonstrated that self-compassionate individuals exhibit greater emotional resilience and psychological well-being.

How someone is raised and the experiences they encounter throughout their lives informs how they see and feel about themselves. A person raised with criticism with be self-critical when they experience problems or setbacks; after all they were blamed and held accountable as little powerless children by adults who themselves may have experienced harsh parenting.

Identifying the kind of self-talk going on in the background is a powerful way to identify, challenge and change negative and detrimental scripts. Words have immense power and how we speak to ourselves affects us more deeply than can be imagined.

Chapter 7: The Power of Positive Thinking

A study carried out by Dr Masaru Emoto (1999) a Japanese scientist interested in the impact of human consciousness on molecules found staggering results from the impact of words on the ability of water molecules to form perfect crystals. He claimed that water exposed to positive thoughts, words, and emotions formed beautiful, symmetrical crystals, while water exposed to negative influences formed disordered, asymmetrical shapes.

Whilst Dr Emoto's work has been criticised, it nonetheless highlights how powerful words and environments are and importantly, invites us to ask if negativity affects water molecules in a lab, what is it doing to a human body that is made up of approximately 60% water?

Therefore, by treating oneself with the same warmth and compassion afforded to others, individuals can cultivate a sense of inner security and self-worth. Therapeutic interventions can help to counter negativity bias by promoting awareness of thought patterns, actively challenging negative beliefs, and cultivating positivity.

One of the common issues that presents itself repeatedly in my work is clients' self-criticism and hostility towards themselves. Sometimes it is jarring to hear clients deride themselves over minor infractions that normally wouldn't warrant acknowledgment. This, and the manner in which a client is speaking to themselves often highlights how they have been treated in the past by primary care givers and significant others and what kind of behaviour has been modelled to them.

Emily, a highly accomplished Investment Banker in a male-dominated field, came to see me after struggling with Imposter Syndrome, self-criticism and significant negativity bias. It took a few sessions to witness how Emily spoke to herself especially under extreme stress.

The work revolved around making and encouraging Emily to become aware of her critical scripts. These were anchored in trauma from an old-fashioned, patriarchal father who had discounted and dismissed Emily's very exitance let alone her achievements and had wanted her to marry and have a family. As a result of such behaviour, Emily has internalised her father's abusive criticisms and believed that she was unworthy, incompetent and struggled with inadequacy despite evidence to the contrary.

Through empathic understanding, unconditional positive regard and inviting Emily to challenge the negative scripts and replace them with those that were loving, kind and compassionate, she slowly rewrote and rewired the way she communicated with herself. This wasn't an easy task for her as she had been used to repeating the harsh criticisms she'd heard growing up, the only difference now was that Emily was doing her fathers job for him.

Over the course of our work, she used unsent letters to stand up to her father by expressing and owning her rage at the injustices she had faced. She also used the same to write to her inner self and offer herself compassion and kindness which she found excruciating.

By embracing imperfection and acknowledging common humanity, individuals can challenge and transcend self-criticism, embrace their inherent worthiness and reclaim their lives.

Summary

In this chapter, we explored the science of positivity and its profound effects on performance and impact on well-being. From neuroscience to psychology, evidence underscores the transformative power of positive thinking. By embracing gratitude practices, cognitive restructuring, mindfulness meditation and positive affirmations, individuals can cultivate a resilient mindset grounded in optimism and self-efficacy. Moreover, by overcoming negativity bias through reframing failure as feedback, seeking social support, and practising self-compassion, individuals can navigate life's challenges with grace and resilience.

Self Reflection Questions:

1. Reflect on a recent setback or challenge you faced. How did you initially interpret the situation, and how might reframing it in a more positive light influence your subsequent actions?
2. Experiment with a gratitude journal for one week, recording three things you're thankful for each day. Notice any shifts in your mood or outlook over the course of the week. What insights did you gain from this practice?
3. Consider a recurring negative thought pattern you've identified in yourself. How might cognitive restructuring techniques help you challenge and

reframe this pattern to cultivate a more positive mindset?

Bibliography

1. Baumeister, R. F., & Leary, M. R. (1995). The need to belong: Desire for interpersonal attachments as a fundamental human motivation. Psychological Bulletin, 117(3), 497–529.
2. Beck, J. S., Beck, A. T., & Dozois, D. J. (2015). Cognitive therapy: Basics and beyond. Guilford Publications.
3. Brown, H. D., Leach, S., Tait, R., & Strugnell, C. (2022). Positive affect and dopamine: A systematic review of the literature. Neuroscience & Biobehavioural Reviews, 134, 1285-1294.
4. Davidson, R. J. (2010). Empirical explorations of mindfulness: Conceptual and methodological conundrums. Emotion, 10(1), 8–11.
5. Dweck, C. S. (2006). Mindset: The new psychology of success. Random House.
6. Emmons, R. A., & McCullough, M. E. (2003). Counting blessings versus burdens: Experimental studies of gratitude and subjective well-being in daily life. Journal of Personality and Social Psychology, 84(2), 377–389.
7. Fredrickson, B. L. (2009). Positivity: Groundbreaking research reveals how to embrace the hidden strength of positive emotions, overcome negativity, and thrive. Crown.
8. Hardy, L., & Jones, G. (2014). Stress, performance, and wellbeing in elite athletes. In Applied sport psychology: Personal growth to peak performance (pp. 340-367). Routledge.
9. Kabat-Zinn, J. (2003). Mindfulness-based interventions in context: Past, present, and future. Clinical Psychology: Science and Practice, 10(2), 144–156.
10. Lebra, T. S. (1976). Shame and guilt: A psycho-cultural perspective. In P. B. Pedersen & M. Kim (Eds.), Cross-cultural perspectives in introductory psychology (pp. 276-293). Kendall/Hunt Publishing Company.
11. Luthans, F., & Youssef, C. M. (2007). Emerging positive organisational behaviour. Journal of Management, 33(3), 321–349.
12. Neff, K. D. (2003). Self-compassion: An alternative conceptualization of a healthy attitude toward oneself. Self and Identity, 2(2), 85–101.
13. Tangney, J. P., & Dearing, R. L. (2002). Shame and guilt. Guilford Press.
14. Wood, J. V., & Perunovic, W. Q. E. (2009). Positive self-statements: Power for some, peril for others. Psychological Science, 20(7), 860–866.

Further Reading

1. Csikszentmihalyi, M. (2008). Flow: The psychology of optimal experience. Harper Perennial Modern Classics.

2. Duckworth, A. (2016). Grit: The power of passion and perseverance. Scribner.
3. Duckworth, A., & Gross, J. J. (2014). Self-control and grit: Related but separable determinants of success. Current Directions in Psychological Science, 23(5), 319–325.
4. Gilbert, D. (2007). Stumbling on happiness. Vintage.
5. Goleman, D. (1995). Emotional intelligence. Bantam Books.
6. Haidt, J. (2006). The happiness hypothesis: Putting ancient wisdom to the test of modern science. Basic Books.
7. Hanson, R. (2013). Hardwiring happiness: The new brain science of contentment, calm, and confidence. Harmony.
8. Lyubomirsky, S. (2008). The how of happiness: A scientific approach to getting the life you want. Penguin.
9. Seligman, M. E. P. (2002). Authentic happiness: Using the new positive psychology to realize your potential for lasting fulfilment. Free Press.
10. Seligman, M. E. P. (2011). Flourish: A visionary new understanding of happiness and well-being. Free Press.

Chapter 8: Managing Anxiety in Uncertain Times

Helping Leaders to Help Those They Manage

In the post-COVID workplace characterised by rapid change and unpredictability, anxiety has emerged as a pervasive issue affecting employees across various industries. As entrepreneurs and organisations grapple with economic turbulence, detrimental and frankly, terrifying political decisions, technological disruptions and global crises, understanding the manifestations of anxiety and its profound impact on individual and employee well-being is crucial.

In this chapter, we delve into the intricacies of work-related anxiety, its effects on individuals and teams, and strategies that entrepreneur-leaders and managers can employ to provide meaningful support.

Understanding Anxiety in the Workplace

Work related anxiety is a multifaceted phenomenon rooted in the complex interplay of biopsychosocial i.e. biological, psychological, social and environmental factors that inform and impact an individual's life. Leka et al (2020), found that work related *and* workplace anxiety encompasses a range of emotional, cognitive and behavioural responses triggered by perceived threats or stressors. These responses may manifest as physical symptoms such as increased heart rate, muscle tension, or gastrointestinal distress as discussed in Chapter 1.

Anxiety can precipitate emotional distress, including feelings of apprehension, worry, or fear, which hinder an individual's ability to focus and engage effectively in their work (Milne et al, 2020). This is further exacerbated with the presence of additional pressure from unreasonable and unattainable expectations or demands from employers or significant others. For example, the lack of support with workload or understanding from employers when an employee is struggling may create an atmosphere of resentment and additional stress.

Recognising that individuals are multifaceted and function on many levels in multiple capacities as opposed to robots programmed to complete specific tasks in a given time is not only important but essential if an organisation wants to thrive and survive. Overloading and thereby, overstressing members of staff creates a toxic work environment. It is wise to remember that we are not yet that far removed from our hunter-gatherer ancestors and have not evolved to work around the clock.

Cognitive impairment such as brain fog and an inability to 'think clearly' or focus on tasks resulting from anxiety caused by overwhelm can impair decision-making processes and problem-solving abilities, leading to suboptimal performance and productivity outcomes (Brosschot et al, 2005). This can have a cyclical effect of frustration and exhaustion from forcing oneself to try to think clearly when the brain is overloaded, exhausted and cannot take on anything more.

I experienced this personally working for an international Employee Assistance Programme. One particular day, I'd dealt with three back to back calls about sexual assault, the clients were very distressed and clearly traumatised. I was exhausted from struggling with early starts at the job because I had chronic insomnia, the strange staff dynamics where I just didn't seem to get on with the cliques and was also personally supporting someone who stated they'd also been the victim of an assault. It was later found that they had fabricated the whole experience and I had been duped. I was deeply traumatised and devastated with this lie.

Coming off the final call, I attempted to write up my case notes and found, terrifyingly, that I couldn't make sense of the letters on my keyboard and I couldn't spell 'and'. I was having a breakdown caused by burnout. My brain had warned me for months but I had ignored it, most of the things described in chapter 1 were clearly present. I had had a sense of extreme panic because I didn't know what was happening, all I remember thinking was 'I NEED my brain for my job!'. I remember getting my things including my car keys and walking out of the office.

Very luckily for me, the receptionist was a First-Aider and had watched me walk by like a zombie, later telling me she'd shouted out as we usually shared raucous banter, and that in this instance, I hadn't heard her. She'd decided to come out of her office and check on me and had immediately taken my keys from my hand and ended up taking me straight to the Royal London Hospital where I was rigged up to several machines and underwent many tests.

Many hours later and way past Loretta's home time, the Consultant sat with me in a corridor as HEMS wheeled a critical patient from a road traffic accident unconscious and covered in blood past us at eye level. He told me off which in hindsight was amusing and *quite* out of order, but necessary and simply told me 'Miss Raithatha, whatever it is that has gotten you to this state needs to stop immediately because you won't be so lucky next time'. Apparently, my symptoms pointed to a high risk of having a stroke. I was only 36, alone and with no support. I was also being catfished before I knew what catfishing was which had devastated my health, sanity and self-confidence and the lie of being abused.

It was six months before I returned to work as my GP refused to sign me fit for work, because I wasn't. Staring at train tracks to and from work wondering what would happen if I jumped was not healthy at all. I wasn't always lucky enough to drive into work but the simple choice of taking my car to work had made a drastic difference to my mental health and ability to cope that day because I hadn't had to navigate public transport.

Chapter 8: Managing Anxiety in Uncertain Times

Luckily, I could rely on sick pay, however the fear and guilt of being off sick exacerbated my recovery. I was on my own, away from family and had lost most friends after coming out. The fear and guilt of being seen outside the house, even to get some groceries was overwhelming. So, I hid inside, venturing out for the briefest periods. I was rebuilding my brain slowly with the help of my therapist and sheer will-power. I found out later that colleagues were told not to contact me. The irony was that I had helped thousands of clients going through exactly this behaviour from their employers!

To this day I am staggered about this behaviour from a company that provided counselling assessments and referrals for many tens of thousands of employees just like me, but didn't have the integrity to look after its own. What struck me was that fellow employees *weren't* treated with the same *persona non grata* status when they were off sick, often recovering from drinking too much or coming down from drug binges. I wonder why I was ringfenced for this treatment?

Mine is by no means an isolated incident. One of the reasons for this book is my work with many thousands of employees from all industries and from all levels of internal hierarchies who have experienced what I did with stress and burnout. Their inability to focus and act fast can have devastating consequences for workers in certain areas of industry such as for machine operators, emergency responders, healthcare professionals and paramedics who experience significantly high levels of stress because of their roles and where their ability to be focused and able to make critical decisions could be a matter of life or death.

Similarly, for entrepreneurs the ability to be resilient in the face of stress and anxiety caused by the changing landscape of entrepreneurship can feel overwhelming and impact as well as hamper progress. Anxiety-induced behavioural changes such as avoidance, procrastination, or seeking constant reassurance from colleagues or managers can exacerbate workplace challenges and strain interpersonal relationships (Nieuwenhuijsen et al., 2019). Similar is true for friends and partners.

The Impact of Anxiety on Employees

The ramifications of workplace anxiety extend beyond individual well-being to encompass broader organisational, business dynamics and outcomes. Research suggests that heightened anxiety levels among employees correlate with decreased productivity, increased absenteeism, presenteeism and higher turnover rates (Cherry, Blanchard, & Brown, 2021).

Jackie a senior advisor with an exemplary track record found herself on a disciplinary which left her shocked and bewildered. When we explored what was going on, she shared that her relationship had suddenly ended and that her father had passed away within weeks. Jackie was left traumatised at the loss of two of the most important relationships in her world.

She had informed her manager and had had a brief period of statutory leave that she spent trying to

Chapter 8: Managing Anxiety in Uncertain Times

organise a funeral and make sense of her partner's decisions to leave without a discussion. She was then expected to return to full duties. Jackie realised that she was in no shape to be at work but wasn't able to have any time off due to punitive policies that would have put her on the path to disciplinaries and eventually, dismissal despite the issues not being her fault.

Through a lack of choice, Jackie forced herself to show up at work, known as presenteeism, but was unable to function as well as she had been before. She was shocked to see that none of her colleagues asked her how she was or offered her any form of support. Her targets were impacted and she felt ambivalent and apathetic towards her clients and organisation. She'd had no time to process the catastrophic losses she'd experienced and didn't have much support outside of work as she had dedicated herself to her work, partner and dad.

As time went by, Jackie found herself getting increasingly anxious and distressed, whilst also struggling with insomnia. She had lost her appetite due to the grief and shock and was drinking more to cope. Jackie realised she had hit rock bottom when she found herself sneaking alcohol into work and taking swigs throughout the day from a water bottle.

The cognitive impairments associated with the overwhelm caused by grief, shock, bereavement and anxiety that Jackie experienced clearly contributed to desperate and perhaps ill-judged decision-making.

Anxiety-induced stressors can lead to burnout and psychological distress, posing significant risks to entrepreneurial and employee mental and physical health (Harvey, 2020). Research has found that the presence of sustained stress and anxiety impacts performance and hinders innovation, impeding organisational adaptability and resilience (Ashford, Lee, & Bobko, 2019). A person would struggle to indulge in creativity when burdened with worry and overwhelm.

Chronic exposure to workplace anxiety has been linked to an array of adverse health outcomes, including cardiovascular disease, insomnia, and compromised immune functioning (Schaufeli & Taris, 2014). Consequently, addressing anxiety in the workplace is imperative not only for enhancing individual well-being but also for fostering a thriving and sustainable business outcome. This is particularly important for entrepreneurs expecting to grow their business and workforce.

Supporting Employees Through Uncertainty

Leaders and managers play a pivotal role in contributing to the atmosphere in the workplace and navigating the complexities of workplace anxiety, through creating supportive environments conducive to employee well-being and resilience.

Demonstrating authentic leadership, including owning failures and embracing some level of vulnerability and modelling adaptive coping behaviours instils confidence and trust among employees, fostering a sense of collective efficacy and resilience (Zacher & Rudolph, 2021).

Conversely, bad managers can create havoc leading to ill-feeling, apprehension and animosity causing employees to feel unsafe, disengaged and despondent due to the subconscious level of threat and fight or flight symptoms they experience on a daily basis, not knowing where the threat is but being aware that it exists. This is no different to out ancestor Dave being out in the wild anticipating being pounced upon by a dangerous predator without warning. Today, the predator is the toxic management and the organisation that refuses to acknowledge they have an issue.

Such toxic and damaging environments are easy to spot; they are often the ones with a high turnover because people are deeply unhappy, detest coming to work and are increasingly utilising their power of choice to move to other departments or leave altogether. Additionally, it is the leaders and managers who are in regular contact with the employee and therefore, not only responsible for, but the ideal individuals to ensure that their reports feel safe and comfortable enough to seek support and guidance as required.

Equally, it is the responsibility of the organisation to foster this sense of safely and reliability by creating a safe space for managers to be educated, feel supported and encouraged to thrive. Every individual in the leadership chain of command needs to be cognisant and literate in empathic leadership that seeks to guide, nurture and support employees by appropriate, respectful communication. This is possible only when they themselves create an environment that models, promotes and champions the psychological safety of each member of staff. The adage of the rotten apple is true here, one bad apple does spoil them all.

Drawing upon evidence-based practices and psychological principles, organisations can implement various strategies to support employees through uncertainty:

Promoting Open Communication

Establishing channels for transparent and empathetic communication enables employees to voice their concerns and seek support without fear of stigma or reprisal (Bergström et al., 2018). Clear, respectful communication is key in any business, being able to convey concepts, ideas, needs and problems is imperative.

Consider this:

1. What kind of work environment do you need, including the type and frequency of support to help you enjoy your work and thrive?
2. Compared to this ideal, how would you identify your current situation?
3. How likely are you to share the shortcomings with your manager, and how likely are they to support your request?
4. Likewise, as a manager, how equipped do you feel to have meaningful conversations that enable you to create a happy workplace?
5. How strong are your boundaries for example? How empathic would you say you were?
6. To what extent would your staff agree or disagree with your assessment of yourself?

Chapter 8: Managing Anxiety in Uncertain Times

Being a leader is an ongoing commitment to learn and grow as a person and as someone who manages others. One rule is to be aware that the circumstances of another's life like Jackie a few pages back, cannot be known. However, offering a kind word or even making her a cup of tea or coffee would have helped her to feel seen and not so alone and devastated in her grief. Strong support procedures may have helped Jackie to manage her response to grief and trauma more mindfully rather than from chronic overwhelm.

Let's look at another case study: Donna was referred to me via an EAP. She had been signed off work after her manager left abruptly at a critical time of year and the data collection and reporting for the entire department was left to Donna. The organisation had been floundering for months under the manager who spent a great deal of time out of the office and in 'meetings' with Donna who often found herself covering for her with senior management.

Because Donna reported to her manager and because of the manager's regular absence, Donna became overwhelmed with trying to do her own work *and* that of her manager that had been delegated to her. Despite trying to tell her manager how she felt, she was belittled frequently, made to feel incompetent and strongly believed that if she pushed things too far, she might lose her job, something she couldn't afford to do.

Eventually, she had woken up one morning and broken down into uncontrollable tears and felt utter despair being unable to get herself motivated enough to go into the office. The same had happened over coming days and eventually she managed to speak to her GP who recognised symptoms of burnout and signed Donna off for a month, much to her horror.

Providing Access to Resources

Offering comprehensive mental health resources, including counselling services, stress management workshops, and self-help materials, empowers employees to proactively address anxiety-related challenges (Väänänen et al., 2020). When her company's HR was made aware of Donna's situation, they referred her for counselling through their Employee Assistance Programme. Here, despite very limited number of sessions she was given, Donna was able to open up and share her fury and disgust about her manager's behaviour and frequent absences and the fact that she could 'swan off whenever she pleased and dump everything on my shoulders! I'm not getting paid to do her job as well as mine, but if I say anything I'm the one that will get into trouble and lose my job!'

I have heard this many thousands of times from staff in all industries. During the sessions, Donna was able to release the anger and helplessness she felt through talking, but also through doing many of the exercises described in this book. We explored how she could address her concerns through the appropriate channels at work by investigating what her rights were through the organisation's policies and procedures and where necessary, to seek external legal advice.

Implementing Flexible and Remote Working Arrangements

These have proven to be life-changing since the lockdown and have shown that contrary to employer's beliefs that employees will be significantly less productive if not watched over by leadership, they have instead, flourished. Whilst the change was sudden and unexpected, organisations realised that in order to survive they needed to adapt and fast. Employees likewise, had to do the same.

What emerged was the fact that employees benefitted significantly from remote and flexible working because they could work around other obligations such as childcare, didn't have the overwhelming stress and the financial and time cost of travelling to and from work, which allowed them more time to do the work without first needing to calm down from the stress of the journey. Another benefit was employees could work from any location therefore enabling organisations to recruit talent from around the world. Employees also saved money they'd have spent on a business wardrobe, lunches, car maintenance and reduce the impact of their travel on the environment.

Therefore, for the organisations still engaged in tussles with demanding employees work from the office for some time during the week, the question is why? What difference does it make? Embracing flexible work policies, such as remote work options and flexible booking systems for appointments, etc., accommodates employees' diverse needs and promotes work-life balance (Allen et al., 2015). Not only does such an accommodation support staff, but can no doubt reduce stress-related sickness absence and presenteeism.

Fostering a Culture of Self-Care:

Whether you are an established business or just engaging in the world of entrepreneurship, focus on and importance for self-care is paramount. Engaging in, and encouraging self-care in your staff, colleagues and networking buddies is very important because nothing works unless you do. Therefore, embracing, adopting and encouraging self-care practices, such as mindfulness meditation, physical exercise, and relaxation techniques, fosters resilience and enhances employees' ability to manage stress effectively (Hülsheger et al., 2015).

Emotional Freedom Techniques (EFT) / Tapping

One innovative approach to managing workplace anxiety is Emotional Freedom Techniques (EFT), commonly referred to as Tapping. Grounded in principles of traditional Chinese medicine and modern psychology, EFT involves gently tapping on specific acupressure points while focusing on distressing emotions or thoughts. Research suggests that EFT can effectively reduce anxiety levels by alleviating psychological distress and promoting emotional regulation (Sebastian & Nelms, 2017).

EFT Tapping Routine for Managing Anxiety:

Identify the Issue: Begin by identifying the specific aspect of anxiety you want to address, such as fear of uncertainty or overwhelming stress.

Then give it a score between 0-10 to indicate how much it

is affecting you. 0 being not at all, and 10 being it is taking over my life.

Setup Statement: Create a setup statement while tapping on the side of the palm with your opposite hand – (the Karate chop point). This statement tells the body what you are aiming to work on, in this case, anxiety, and acknowledges the issue while affirming self-acceptance and empowerment. For example, 'Even though I feel anxious about the uncertainty at work, I deeply and completely accept myself.'

Tap on Acupressure Points: Tap on each of the following acupressure points while repeating your setup statement or a shortened reminder phrase such as 'I deeply and completely accept myself,' or 'I am safe and all is well':

- Spot between the eyebrows
- Side of the eye
- Under the eye
- Under the nose
- Chin
- Collarbone
- Top of the head

Repeat and Reflect
Continue tapping on the acupressure points while repeating your setup statement or reminder phrase. Pay attention to any shifts in your feelings or sensations.

Assess and Re-evaluate
After completing several rounds of tapping, assess your anxiety levels and any changes in your emotional state; what score would you select now? If necessary, repeat the

tapping sequence or adjust your setup statement to address any remaining issues. Most people find that tapping releases emotion and they find themselves tearful this is a great sign and nothing to be concerned about. As you are tapping on meridian points, blockages are released and you may feel different including tired, angry, tearful, etc., while your body comes back into balance. Be gentle with yourself.

By incorporating EFT tapping into their self-care routine, individuals can effectively manage anxiety and build resilience in the face of uncertainty.

Summary
Uncertainty in the workplace whether as an entrepreneur or employee can be daunting and managing anxiety in uncertain times requires a multifaceted approach grounded in empathy, evidence-based practices, and proactive leadership. Clearly, with the right support and coping strategies, individuals can navigate anxiety with resilience and confidence. Leaders, managers, mentors, support networks can all play a crucial and significant role in creating a supportive environment that fosters well-being and empowers employees to thrive, even in uncertain times. By addressing anxiety head-on, implementing supportive measures and promoting effective coping strategies like EFT tapping, Mindfulness, organisations can cultivate a culture of resilience and adaptability that enables both individual and collective success.

Equally, through fostering open communication, providing access to resources, and promoting self-care initiatives, organisations can cultivate a culture of resilience that empowers employees to navigate workplace challenges with confidence and adaptability. Furthermore, integrating innovative techniques such as EFT tapping can offer additional support in managing anxiety and enhancing overall well-being in the workplace.

Self Reflection Questions:
1. What specific situations or aspects of my entrepreneurial journey trigger anxiety for me and why do they have this effect?
2. How does my anxiety impact my decision-making process and ability to take calculated risks in my business?
3. What coping mechanisms or strategies have I found effective in managing my anxiety and how can I integrate them more consistently into my daily routine as an entrepreneur?

Bibliography
1. Allen, T. D., Johnson, R. C., Kiburz, K. M., & Shockley, K. M. (2015). Work-Family Conflict and Flexible Work Arrangements: Deconstructing Flexibility. Personnel Psychology, 68(2), 225–258.
2. Ashford, S. J., Lee, C., & Bobko, P. (2019). Content, Causes, and Consequences of Job Insecurity: A Theory-Based Measure and Meta-Analytic Examination. Academy of Management Journal, 62(1), 203–226.
3. Bergström, G., Bodin, L., Hagberg, J., Aronsson, G., & Josephson, M. (2018). Sickness Presenteeism Today, Sickness Absenteeism Tomorrow? A Prospective Study on Sickness Presenteeism and Future Sickness Absence. BMC Public Health, 18(1), 224.
4. Brosschot, J. F., Pieper, S., & Thayer, J. F. (2005). Expanding Stress Theory: Prolonged Activation and Perseverative Cognition. Psychoneuroendocrinology, 30(10), 1043–1049.

5. Cherry, M. A., Blanchard, A. L., & Brown, L. V. (2021). The Influence of Job Insecurity and Job Stress on the Turnover Intentions of Federal Employees in the United States. Public Personnel Management, 50(1), 3–28.
6. Grant, A. M., & Ashford, S. J. (2008). The Dynamics of Proactivity at Work. Research in Organisational Behaviour, 28, 3–34.
7. Harvey, S. (2020). Employee Stress and Mental Health: Causes, Impacts, and Solutions. Human Resource Management International Digest, 28(1), 3–6.
8. Hülsheger, U. R., Alberts, H. J., Feinholdt, A., & Lang, J. W. (2015). Benefits of Mindfulness at Work: The Role of Mindfulness in Emotion Regulation, Emotional Exhaustion, and Job Satisfaction. Journal of Applied Psychology, 100(2), 310–325.
9. Kahn, W. A. (1990). Psychological Conditions of Personal Engagement and Disengagement at Work. Academy of Management Journal, 33(4), 692–724.
10. Lazarus, R. S., & Folkman, S. (1984). Stress, Appraisal, and Coping. Springer Publishing Company.
11. Leka, S., Jain, A., Iavicoli, S., & Di Tecco, C. (2020). An Evaluation of the Policy Context on Psychosocial Risks and Mental Health in the Workplace in the European Union: Achievements, Challenges, and the Future. Safety Science, 128, 104729.
12. Milne, L. C., Thorsteinsson, E. B., & MacKinnon, C. R. (2020). A Comprehensive Evaluation of the Factors Contributing to the Development and Maintenance of Anxiety and Depression in Distressed University Students. Journal of Affective Disorders, 263, 549–557.
13. Nieuwenhuijsen, K., Bruinvels, D., Frings-Dresen, M., & Sluiter, J. (2019). The Effects of Work-Related and Individual Factors on the Work Ability Index: A Systematic Review. Occupational and Environmental Medicine, 66(4), 211–220.
14. Schaufeli, W. B., & Taris, T. W. (2014). A Critical Review of the Job Demands-Resources Model: Implications for Improving Work and Health. In G. F. Bauer & O. Hämmig (Eds.), Bridging Occupational, Organisational and Public Health (pp. 43–68). Springer.
15. Seligman, M. E. P. (2018). Learned Optimism: How to Change Your Mind and Your Life. Vintage.
16. Selye, H. (1956). The Stress of Life. McGraw-Hill Education.
17. Siegrist, J. (1996). Adverse Health Effects of High-Effort/Low-Reward Conditions. Journal of Occupational Health Psychology, 1(1), 27–41.
18. Smit, B. W., Eling, P. A., & Coenen, A. M. (2021). The Role of Leaders in Creating Psychologically Safe Work Environments: A Literature Review. Safety Science, 133, 105007.

19. Sonnentag, S., & Fritz, C. (2015). Recovery from Job Stress: The Role of Unwinding and Psychological Detachment. Journal of Applied Psychology, 100(5), 1209–1222.
20. Tugade, M. M., & Fredrickson, B. L. (2004). Resilient Individuals Use Positive Emotions to Bounce Back from Negative Emotional Experiences. Journal of Personality and Social Psychology, 86(2), 320–333.
21. Wright, T. A., & Cropanzano, R. (2000). Psychological Well-Being and Job Satisfaction as Predictors of Job Performance. Journal of Occupational Health Psychology, 5(1), 84–94.

Chapter 9: Embracing Failure as a Stepping Stone to Success

Failure is not just an inevitable part of the entrepreneurial journey, but of life itself. Every individual has failed numerous times and overcome failure even more times. Consider how many times you failed as a baby trying to speak or walk? It was frustrating, but at the time your young self hadn't attached any meaning or value to either outcome. There was an inherent desire to move, learn to sit upright, then crawl, and finally, walk. It was that simple.

Unfortunately, during the lifespan, each individual learns what psychologists refer to as *conditions of worth*. Simply put, we are celebrated IF we meet a parent's or care-giver's need for validation otherwise we experience a set of reprimands or various forms of withdrawal or abandonment which feel like catastrophic rejection to little beings and cause great harm. Think about the people you know that might refer to themselves as 'people pleasers', often exhausted, secretly resentful and frequently verging on burnout, but who *still* continue to please regardless of the cost to their own well-being.

I recently observed a young woman barely in the twenties in a fast-food restaurant continuously ply her tiny tot with sugar-laden foodstuff and drink and then demanded the child offer gratitude. When the child, barely old enough to walk, didn't respond, (why would they?), and refused to participate in this self-congratulatory and aggrandising behaviour, it was threatened with punishment of being taken home immediately. As the child continued to, well, be a child, mum became increasingly incensed taking the child's not telling her how much of a 'good mummy' she was, referred to as a lack of positive strokes as rejection.

Many individuals have experienced this kind of interaction in some alliteration throughout their childhood which has impacted their sense of self-worth, failure and their relationship with themselves, others and their world as a result. Yet, it is not the failure itself that defines us, but rather how we respond to it.

In this chapter, we will explore the shifting perspectives on failure, its role in entrepreneurship, and strategies for learning from failure to bounce back stronger. We will delve into overcoming the fear of failure and embracing risk-taking as essential components of incorporating teachings from wisdom gained in ancient conflicts and how to relate them to modern entrepreneurial success.

Shifting Perspectives on Failure

In many cultures, failure is stigmatised as something to be avoided at all costs. However, successful entrepreneurs are those who are able to accept that failure is an essential

Chapter 9: Embracing Failure as a Stepping Stone to Success

and necessary part of success.

In the Shrimad Bhagavad Gita, a revered Hindu scripture, Lord Krishna advises Arjuna, a prince from a mighty dynasty, to detach himself from the outcomes of his actions during an epic battle against members of his own extended family and focus on the process explaining that Arjuna must understand that failure is not the opposite of success but rather a stepping stone towards it.

Arjuna's doubts stem from various factors. Firstly, he is deeply troubled by the thought of fighting against his own relatives, teachers, and friends who are standing on the opposing side of the battlefield. Entrepreneurship can elicit similar feelings when forced to go against the thoughts and feelings of family for example.

He is also troubled by the consequences of the war, fearing the destruction it will bring upon his own family and society as a whole. Additionally, Arjuna is conflicted about the righteousness of the war itself, questioning whether it is truly justifiable to engage in such a violent conflict.

In this moment of crisis, Lord Krishna, who serves as Arjuna's charioteer, imparts divine wisdom to him through the Bhagavad Gita. Shri Krishna reminds Arjuna of his duty as a warrior and a member of the warrior class (Kshatriya), emphasising the importance of fulfilling one's responsibilities without attachment to the outcomes. He teaches Arjuna about the concepts of dharma (duty and righteousness) and karma (action), urging him to perform his duty as a warrior without being swayed by personal desires or attachments.

This perspective shift allows individuals to view failure as a natural part of the journey rather than a final destination. However, work on challenging negative self-belief and acceptance needs to be undertaken in order to achieve this level of equanimity,

Similarly, in the Mahabharata, the epic tale of ancient India during which the Bhagavat Gita was imparted to the world, we see numerous examples of characters facing failure and adversity. Yudhishthira's loss at the game of dice is a pivotal moment in the Mahabharata, leading to significant consequences for him and his family. Yudhishthira, the eldest of the Pandava brothers, is known for his integrity, righteousness, and sense of dharma.

During a game of dice, Yudhishthira becomes ensnared in a cunning plot orchestrated by Shakuni, the uncle of the Kauravas. Shakuni manipulates the game using loaded dice, ensuring that Yudhishthira loses everything, including his kingdom, wealth, including his brothers and himself, who are forced into exile for thirteen years.

Despite the unjust circumstances of his loss and betrayal, Yudhishthira accepts the outcome with stoicism and dignity. He upholds his dharma as a Kshatriya (warrior) and a man of honour by abiding by the rules of the game and honouring his word. Despite the intense emotional turmoil and humiliation he experiences, Yudhishthira maintains his composure and refuses to harbour resentment or seek revenge.

Chapter 9: Embracing Failure as a Stepping Stone to Success

Instead, Yudhishthira focuses on fulfilling his responsibilities during the period of exile, demonstrating resilience and fortitude in the face of adversity.

Yudhishthira's loss at dice and subsequent response can be likened to the challenges faced by entrepreneurs in several ways:

Facing Adversity: Like Yudhishthira, entrepreneurs often encounter unexpected setbacks and failures in their ventures, such as financial losses, market downturns, or failed initiatives. Just as Yudhishthira accepted his loss with dignity, entrepreneurs must acknowledge and confront adversity head-on, without succumbing to despair or resentment. Both are a natural part of the entrepreneurial journey and, just like learning to walk as a toddler, can be overcome with patience and resilience.

Resilience and Adaptability: Yudhishthira's ability to endure hardships during his exile reflects the resilience and adaptability required of entrepreneurs. Despite being stripped of his kingdom and comforts, Yudhishthira persevered and adapted to the challenges of forest life because he knew that this situation was temporary and that he would be able to return home one day. Similarly, entrepreneurs must navigate through turbulent times, pivot their strategies and innovate in the moment, in order to survive and thrive in a competitive business environment.

Commitment to Values: Yudhishthira's unwavering commitment to righteousness and integrity serves as a reminder to entrepreneurs to uphold ethical values in their business practices. Despite the temptation to compromise ethics for short-term gains, entrepreneurs who prioritise integrity, have the courage to be vulnerable and honest, build trust with customers, employees, and stakeholders, fostering long-term success and sustainability.

Leadership and Decision-Making: Yudhishthira's role as a leader within his family exemplifies the responsibilities and challenges faced by entrepreneurs in leading their teams and organisations. Like Yudhishthira, entrepreneurs must make tough decisions, often under pressure and uncertainty, while maintaining a sense of clarity, vision, and moral compass to steer their ventures towards success.

Both Arjuna's and Yudhishthira's experiences and responses in the Bhagavad Gita and Mahabharata respectively, offer valuable lessons for entrepreneurs, highlighting the importance of resilience, integrity, adaptability, and ethical leadership in overcoming challenges and achieving long-term success in the business world.

Another revered book, the Tao Te Ching, an ancient Chinese text attributed to the sage Lao Tzu, teaches the concept of **Wu-Wei**, or effortless action. This philosophy suggests that by embracing the natural flow of life, including both successes and failures, we can achieve harmony and balance.

The concept of Wu-Wei, emphasises the idea of "effortless action" or "non-doing." In the context of entrepreneurial well-being, Wu-Wei can offer valuable insights and practices to enhance productivity, creativity, and overall mental health:

Flow State: Wu-Wei encourages individuals to find a state of flow, where actions are spontaneous, effortless, and aligned with the natural flow of events. Entrepreneurs who embrace Wu-Wei strive to work in a state of flow, where they are fully immersed in their tasks, experiencing a sense of deep focus, enjoyment and fulfilment. This state of flow not only enhances productivity but also promotes a sense of well-being and satisfaction.

Adaptability: Wu-Wei teaches the importance of being *adaptable* and *responsive* to changing circumstances, rather than rigidly adhering to fixed plans or strategies. Entrepreneurs who practice Wu-Wei remain open to new opportunities, embrace uncertainty, and adapt their actions based on the ever-changing business landscape. By cultivating a mindset of flexibility and spontaneity, entrepreneurs can navigate challenges more effectively and maintain a sense of equilibrium amidst uncertainty.

Stress Reduction: Wu-Wei encourages individuals to let go of unnecessary striving and resistance, leading to reduced stress and anxiety. Entrepreneurs often face high levels of stress due to the demands of running a business, making important decisions, and dealing with uncertainty. By adopting a Wu-Wei approach, entrepreneurs can learn to let go of excessive control, trust in the natural unfolding of events and find greater ease and peace of mind in their entrepreneurial endeavours.

Intuition and Creativity: Wu-Wei emphasises the importance of tapping into one's intuition and creativity, rather than relying solely on analytical thinking or forceful action. Entrepreneurs who practice Wu-Wei cultivate a deeper connection with their intuition, allowing them to make decisions from a place of inner wisdom and insight. This fosters innovation, creative problem-solving, and the ability to see opportunities where others may not.

Work-Life Balance: Wu-Wei encourages individuals to cultivate a harmonious balance between work and personal life, avoiding the trap of overwork and burnout. Entrepreneurs who prioritise Wu-Wei recognise the importance of taking breaks, nurturing relationships and engaging in activities that rejuvenate their mind, body, and spirit. By honouring their need for rest and relaxation, entrepreneurs can sustain their well-being and longevity in the entrepreneurial journey.

The concept of Wu-Wei offers entrepreneurs a holistic framework for enhancing well-being, productivity, and resilience in their entrepreneurial pursuits. By embracing the principles of effortless action, adaptability, stress reduction, intuition and work-life balance, entrepreneurs can cultivate a more sustainable and fulfilling entrepreneurial path.

Strategies For Learning from Failure
Cultivate a Growth Mindset
Embrace the belief that intelligence and abilities can be developed through dedication and hard work. View failure

Chapter 9: Embracing Failure as a Stepping Stone to Success

as an opportunity for growth rather than a reflection of your inherent worth.

Practice Self-Compassion
Treat yourself with kindness and understanding in the face of failure. Research by Kristin Neff demonstrates that self-compassion fosters resilience and emotional well-being, enabling individuals to bounce back from setbacks more effectively.

Seek Feedback
Actively solicit feedback from mentors, peers and customers to gain valuable insights into areas for improvement, especially after failure. Constructive feedback provides priceless opportunities for learning and growth. Explore what went wrong for example, and why? Consider how you can intervene and make it better in a way that has a mutually beneficial win:win outcome for all parties involved. This may mean revising what is important to hold onto and what isn't in order to achieve a desired outcome.

Analyse Failure Objectively
Take a step back and analyse the factors that contributed to the failure, focusing on actionable lessons rather than dwelling on blame or self-criticism thereby speeding up the process of reflection and implementation of the new insights gained from the failed task. The practice of post-mortem analysis is heavily incorporated in sports. Chinese athletes employ various strategies to bounce back from defeat. Here are some common approaches they might use:

Resilience and Mental Toughness
Chinese athletes often undergo rigorous mental training to develop resilience and mental toughness. They learn to cope with setbacks, maintain focus and stay motivated despite defeat.

Analysing Performance
After a defeat, Chinese athletes typically engage in a thorough analysis of their performance. They identify areas where they fell short and work on improving their skills and techniques.

Seeking Support
Chinese athletes may seek support from coaches, teammates and sports psychologists to help them process their emotions and regain confidence after a loss. They may also draw inspiration from past victories and the success of their peers.

Setting New Goals
Following a defeat, Chinese athletes often set new goals to refocus their efforts and maintain motivation. They may break down their long-term objectives into smaller, achievable milestones and develop a plan to work towards them. By amalgamating strong mindset growth, performance analysis, seeking support and self-care, entrepreneurs can significantly enhance the opportunities for success and growth.

Adopting a Growth Mindset
Chinese athletes embrace a growth mindset, believing that setbacks are opportunities for learning and growth. They view defeat as a temporary setback and as an opportunity

Chapter 9: Embracing Failure as a Stepping Stone to Success

to regroup and refocus their energies and minds, rather than a permanent failure and use it as motivation to improve and succeed in the future.

Physical Recovery

Chinese athletes prioritise physical recovery after a defeat, allowing their bodies time to rest and recuperate. They may adjust their training routines, focus on injury prevention, and prioritise nutrition and hydration to ensure they are in optimal condition for future competitions.

Overall, Chinese athletes approach defeat with a combination of resilience, self-reflection and determination to learn and improve. They understand that setbacks are a natural part of the athletic journey and use them as opportunities to become stronger and more successful in the long run. Similar approaches adapted in other industries encourage teams to learn from mistakes and prepare for future success.

Set Realistic Expectations

Manage Expectations

Acknowledge that setbacks are a normal part of the entrepreneurial journey. Bandura (1997) best known for his work on social cognitive theory and self-efficacy in the context of goals, emphasises the importance of setting achievable goals to maintain motivation and resilience in the face of failure. Bandura emphasises the importance of an individual's belief in their ability to accomplish a particular task or goal.

Bandura suggests that individuals with high self-efficacy are more likely to set challenging goals for themselves and persist in the face of obstacles. They tend to exert greater effort and show more resilience when pursuing their goals.

For entrepreneurs, Bandura's insights on goals and self-efficacy are highly relevant and clearly translate to the needs and demands posed by entrepreneurship. Like our warriors, kings and athletes, anyone willing to succeed has these important traits as companions.

Setting Challenging Goals
Entrepreneurs with high self-efficacy are more inclined to set ambitious and realistic goals for their ventures. They believe in their ability to overcome challenges and achieve success, motivating them to aim higher and strive for excellence.

Persistence and Resilience
Entrepreneurship is fraught with uncertainty and obstacles. Those with strong self-efficacy are more likely to persevere in the face of setbacks, viewing failures as temporary setbacks rather than insurmountable barriers. This resilience enables them to stay focused on their goals despite adversity.

Effort and Initiative
High self-efficacy entrepreneurs are proactive in taking initiative and investing effort in their ventures. This may translate to accessing and undertaking training, investing in Mentorship and Coaching and regularly exploring strategies to take care of themselves in order to be at the top of their game. They are willing to put in the hard work

Chapter 9: Embracing Failure as a Stepping Stone to Success

and dedication necessary to turn their aspirations into reality. This proactive approach increases their likelihood of success.

Learning From Failure
Bandura's theory suggests that individuals with high self-efficacy are more likely to view failure as a learning opportunity rather than a reflection of their abilities. Similarly, entrepreneurs can leverage setbacks as valuable learning experiences, adapting their strategies and refining their goals based on feedback and reflection.

In essence, Bandura's insights highlight the crucial role of self-efficacy beliefs in shaping entrepreneurial behaviour and outcomes. By fostering a strong sense of self-efficacy, entrepreneurs can set and pursue ambitious goals with confidence, persistence, and resilience, ultimately increasing their chances of success in the dynamic and challenging world of entrepreneurship.

Embrace Change
Adopt an iterative approach to problem-solving, where failure is seen as feedback that informs the next incarnation of your product or service.

Eric Ries (2011) developed **The Lean Startup** methodology, a systematic approach to developing businesses and products. It emphasises rapid iteration, continuous testing, and validated learning to bring a product to market efficiently and effectively. Some key aspects of the Lean Startup methodology include:

Minimum Viable Product (MVP): The Lean Startup encourages the development of a Minimum Viable

Product, which is the simplest version of a product that allows a team to collect the maximum amount of validated learning about customers with the least effort (Ries,). Instead of spending extensive time and resources building a full-featured product, entrepreneurs create a basic version to test their assumptions and gather feedback from early adopters.

Build-Measure-Learn Feedback Loop: The core of the Lean Startup methodology revolves around the *Build*-Measure-Learn feedback loop. It starts with building a MVP, followed by *measuring* how customers *respond* to it, and *learning* from those measurements to inform the next version of the product (Ries, 2011). This iterative process allows startups to quickly adapt to changing market conditions and customer needs.

Validated Learning: Validated learning is about testing hypotheses and validating assumptions through experimentation. Rather than relying solely on intuition or guesswork, Lean Startup advocates for using data and feedback from real users to make informed decisions about product development and business strategy.

Pivot and Persevere: The Lean Startup recognises that not all initial ideas will succeed, and it's **essential** for entrepreneurs to be open to pivoting or persevering based on what they learn from customer feedback which can make or break a business. A pivot involves making a fundamental change to the product or business model in response to validated learning, while perseverance involves doubling down on what's working and iterating further.

Continuous Innovation: The Lean Startup promotes a culture of continuous innovation and improvement. By embracing experimentation and learning, startups can stay agile and adapt quickly to market feedback, enabling them to outmanoeuvre larger, more established competitors (Ries, 2011).

Overall, the Lean Startup methodology provides a structured framework for startups to navigate the uncertainty of building new products and businesses, helping them increase their chances of success in a rapidly changing landscape.

Practice Mindfulness
Cultivate mindfulness practices to amplify present-moment awareness and non-judgmental acceptance of your experiences, including failure. Use both mindfulness, loving kindness and journalling to explore how you can incorporate the Lean Startup Method to your specific offering.

Harness the Power of Storytelling
Share your failures and setbacks with others, reframing them as valuable learning experiences rather than sources of shame. Research in social psychology demonstrates that storytelling fosters connection and empathy, creating opportunities for collective learning and growth. Showing up, owning your story, especially being vulnerable and transparent with failure can help you connect with your audience at a deep level. All our stories are important

because they provide unique and often, creative solutions to problems we may not have considered.

Develop Resilience Skills
Build resilience skills, such as problem-solving, emotional regulation, and social support, to navigate adversity effectively. The resilience framework proposed Seligman (2011) emphasises the importance of optimism, perseverance, and gratitude in overcoming setbacks.

Celebrate Progress
Acknowledge and celebrate small victories along the way, even in the face of failure. Research in positive psychology suggests that cultivating a sense of gratitude and appreciation for progress, however minute, as discussed in earlier chapters fosters resilience and well-being, motivating individuals to persevere despite setbacks.

Overcoming Fear of Failure and Embracing Risk-Taking
Fear of failure is a common barrier that can paralyse individuals and hinder their ability to take necessary risks in entrepreneurship. However, research from various fields provides insights into overcoming this fear and embracing risk-taking as an essential component of success.

One approach to overcoming the fear of failure is to reframe it as a natural and necessary part of the entrepreneurial journey. Dweck's (2006) work on growth mindset suggested that, individuals can shift their perspective by viewing failure as a learning opportunity rather than a reflection of their abilities once again echoing the work of Bandura. By adopting a growth mindset, entrepreneurs can embrace challenges and

Chapter 9: Embracing Failure as a Stepping Stone to Success

setbacks as valuable experiences that contribute to their personal and professional development.

Drawing inspiration from ancient wisdom traditions such as the Bhagavad Gita, entrepreneurs can adopt principles like **karma yoga** to navigate the fear of failure. In karma yoga, individuals focus on the action itself rather than being attached to the outcomes. By detaching themselves from the fear of failure, entrepreneurs can approach risk-taking with a sense of equanimity, allowing them to make decisions based on the merits of the action rather than the potential consequences.

Moreover, research in behavioural economics suggests that individuals tend to overestimate the negative consequences of failure while underestimating the potential benefits of success. This bias, known as **loss aversion**, can lead to a reluctance to take risks. This may be due to previous experiences of difficult and indeed, traumatic losses which inform their level of trepidation in new ventures.

However, by reframing failure as an opportunity for growth and learning, entrepreneurs can mitigate this bias and make more informed decisions about risk-taking. Studies have shown that framing failure as a natural part of the learning process can reduce the aversion to risk and increase willingness to pursue opportunities despite potential setbacks.

In addition to reframing failure, cultivating self-compassion is another effective strategy for overcoming the fear of failure. Research by Neff (2011) demonstrates that self-compassion involves treating oneself with kindness and understanding in the face of failure or adversity. By practicing self-compassion, entrepreneurs can develop resilience and emotional well-being, enabling them to bounce back from setbacks and take risks with confidence.

Summary

We have explored the shifting perspectives on failure and its role in entrepreneurship in this chapter. We discussed strategies for learning from failure, including cultivating a growth mindset, seeking feedback and practicing self-compassion. Additionally, we examined techniques for overcoming the fear of failure and embracing risk-taking, drawing inspiration from ancient wisdom traditions such as the Bhagavad Gita, the Mahabharata and the Tao Te Ching. By incorporating these strategies into their entrepreneurial journey, individuals can navigate failure with resilience and turn setbacks into opportunities for growth and success.

Self Reflection Questions

1. Reflect on a past failure or setback in your entrepreneurial journey. What were the key lessons you learned from this experience?
2. How do you currently approach failure? Are there any mindset shifts or strategies you would like to implement to better embrace failure as a stepping stone to success?
3. Think of a risk you've been hesitant to take in your business. What steps can you take to mitigate the fear of failure and move forward with confidence?

Chapter 9: Embracing Failure as a Stepping Stone to Success

Bibliography

1. Ariely, D. (2009). Predictably Irrational: The Hidden Forces That Shape Our Decisions. HarperCollins.
2. Bhagavad Gita. (Trans. Easwaran, E.). (2007). Nilgiri Press.
3. Brown, B. (2012). Daring Greatly: How the Courage to Be Vulnerable Transforms the Way We Live, Love, Parent, and Lead. Penguin.
4. Duckworth, A. (2016). Grit: The Power of Passion and Perseverance. Scribner.
5. Dweck, C. S. (2006). Mindset: The New Psychology of Success. Random House.
6. Greitens, E. (2015). Resilience: Hard-Won Wisdom for Living a Better Life. Houghton Mifflin Harcourt.
7. McGonigal, K. (2015). The Upside of Stress: Why Stress Is Good for You, and How to Get Good at It. Avery.
8. Neff, K. D. (2011). Self-Compassion: The Proven Power of Being Kind to Yourself. HarperCollins.
9. Ries, E. (2011). The Lean Startup: How Today's Entrepreneurs Use Continuous Innovation to Create Radically Successful Businesses. Crown Business.
10. Seligman, M. E. P. (2011). Flourish: A Visionary New Understanding of Happiness and Well-being. Free Press.
11. Tversky, A., & Kahneman, D. (1991). Loss aversion in riskless choice: A reference-dependent model. The Quarterly Journal of Economics, 106(4), 1039-1061.

Chapter 10: Effective Communication in Business and Life

The Importance of Effective Communication Skills for Business Success

Effective communication is the cornerstone of success in both business and personal relationships. Whether you're conveying ideas to colleagues, negotiating deals with clients, or simply interacting with friends and family, the ability to communicate effectively can significantly impact your outcomes. In this chapter, we'll explore the importance of effective communication skills, strategies for improving verbal and nonverbal communication, active listening techniques, conflict resolution strategies, and delve into the various types of communication, including Non-Violent Communication from the work of Dr Marshall Rosenberg, Mark Goulston and George Kohlreiser.

In the fast-paced world of business, clear and concise communication is vital for success. It ensures that everyone is on the same page, minimises misunderstandings and fosters a collaborative environment. Effective communication skills enable entrepreneurs and leaders to inspire and motivate their teams, facilitate innovation, and drive organisational growth. From delivering persuasive presentations to negotiating deals and resolving conflicts, effective communication is a skill that can elevate individuals and organisations to new heights.

Strategies for Improving Verbal and Nonverbal Communication

Verbal Communication: Clarity and Precision

Using straightforward language is essential for conveying messages without ambiguity. Ambiguous language can lead to misunderstandings and confusion. When communicating, strive to be concise and clear, avoiding unnecessary jargon or complex terminology. Consider the audience's level of understanding and adjust your language accordingly to ensure that your message is easily comprehensible to all recipients.

Active Voice

Employing active voice enhances clarity and assertiveness in communication. Active voice places emphasis on the subject performing the action, making the message more direct and engaging. By using active voice, you can convey your ideas with greater impact and authority. For example, instead of saying 'Mistakes were made,' say 'I made mistakes,' taking ownership of the action and demonstrating accountability. Taking accountability has significant personal benefits including building self-confidence and authority in every situation. Taking ownership of mistakes enhances personal standing with, and respect from others it also models top-level personal conduct and values.

Empathy

Understanding the perspectives of others is crucial for effective communication. Empathy involves putting yourself in the shoes of the recipient and considering their needs, concerns, and emotions. The Sioux proverb that states 'before you judge a person, first walk ten valleys in their moccasins' is a powerful example of empathy in action. None of us can know what is going on for anyone we may be dealing with. The person overtaking you on the road may just be rushing to get to their loved one before they passed away, or attending some emergency we know nothing about. Indeed, they may just be an ignorant fool that might benefit from some anger management classes.

Likewise, the person turning up late to work daily, whilst annoying and frustrating, may be dealing with an ill or dependent child or elderly relative or another situation out of their control. They may be struggling with anxiety or depression. By empathising with others, you can tailor your communication to resonate with them on a deeper level, fostering trust and rapport, acknowledge their feelings and experiences, and respond with sensitivity and understanding. Empathy is a crucial and necessary part of daily life, not just in business transactions. When employed in the pursuit of a mutually favourable outcome, the gift of empathy can create an atmosphere of safety and belonging, making it easier to see and understand each other's viewpoints.

Choosing to respond versus react from an empathic viewpoint in difficult situations can offer a more favourable outcome based on compassion and loving kindness.

Simplify Complex Ideas
Breaking down intricate concepts into digestible chunks is essential for ensuring understanding. Complex ideas can be overwhelming, leading to confusion, disengagement and even disagreement. This is particularly important in relationships, both personal and professional. The reality is, we are all individuals with vastly different perspectives from our unique experience of, and journey through life.

Add to this the fact that the world is increasingly a mix of many blended groups of individuals bringing incredible richness and diversity but also difference in many forms. Most offices, networking and meeting places are populated with individuals from around the globe with different languages, cultures, belief systems, values and visions. Whilst this is an incredible opportunity to learn and grow, things can get complex especially with our capacity for translation and understanding from our personal world view. The more limited an individual's life experience and world view, the lower the capacity to understand, accept and incorporate difference or change.

Chapter 10: Effective Communication in Business and Life

When communicating complex information, strive to simplify it by using analogies, examples, or visual aids to make it more tangible, accessible and understandable to everyone. By presenting information in a clear and structured manner, you can facilitate understanding and retention whilst also being inclusive and empathic around meeting people's different needs.

Feedback Mechanisms
Encouraging feedback from colleagues, partners and friends is vital for gauging understanding and addressing any misconceptions promptly however difficult or uncomfortable this may be. Misconceptions and misunderstandings left to fester can end up being complicated and difficult issues to resolve later and negatively impact the relationship, both personal and professional. Feedback provides valuable insights into how your message is being received and understood by others. Actively seek feedback through open-ended questions, surveys, or one-on-one discussions to ensure that your communication is effective. Use feedback to identify areas for improvement and refine your communication approach accordingly.

Nonverbal Communication:
Body Language Awareness:
Paying attention to body language, including posture, gestures, and facial expressions, is essential for conveying confidence and sincerity. Nonverbal cues can often communicate more than words alone, influencing how your message is perceived by others. Maintain an open and relaxed posture, use gestures to emphasise

key points, and ensure that your facial expressions align with your message to project authenticity and credibility.

You can practice observing and understanding body language by being aware of how people hold themselves when they are speaking with you or others. Being aware of your gut feeling around people can give you more information that can be crucial in your safety, physically, emotionally and financially in business. If something feels wrong, leave.

Eye Contact
Maintaining appropriate eye contact is crucial for establishing rapport and conveying attentiveness. Eye contact communicates engagement and interest in the conversation, fostering connection and trust between communicators. Avoiding or excessive eye contact can signal disinterest or discomfort, so aim for a balance that feels natural and respectful. If the person you are speaking with appears to be distracted or looking everywhere else but at you, check in with them.

For example, 'James, I can't help but notice I don't have your full attention, do you need to go?' This may feel uncomfortable; however, this is your precious time. By calling the behaviour to the individual's attention you are respecting yourself, your time and acknowledging that you are aware of it. You are also giving them the option to address it by offering due attention to the conversation they are having with you, or to stop and leave. This doesn't need to be confrontational but it does provide an opportunity to reset or end a conversation.

Tone and Inflection
Modulating tone and inflection is essential for conveying emotions and emphasis effectively. Your tone of voice can significantly impact how your message is interpreted by others. Pay attention to the intonation, volume, and pace of your speech, adjusting them to match the context and convey the desired emotions. Use variations in tone and inflection to add emphasis to key points and convey sincerity and conviction. If you're unsure about how you come across to people, ask trusted friends for feedback, also become aware of how to speak with others. Are you different when speaking with friends and colleagues? Why and how?

Whom do you admire because of their voice and the way they speak. What specifically do you enjoy about listening to them? To improve the way you speak, again watch and listen to people speak whether in real life or from the many videos available on communication online and slowly change how you present yourself to others and watch their reaction.

Personal Space
Respecting personal boundaries is critical for creating a comfortable and non-threatening environment for communication. Different cultures and individuals have varying expectations regarding personal space, so be mindful of the distance between yourself and others during interactions. Invading someone's personal space

with a pat on the shoulder or touching their arms for example, can be perceived as intrusive or aggressive, while respecting boundaries demonstrates respect and consideration for the other person's comfort. A great many people greet each other with a handshake or hug, however not everyone feels comfortable doing so. It is perfectly acceptable and respectful to ask if they are a hugger or not.

By incorporating these strategies into your verbal and nonverbal communication practices, you can enhance clarity, understanding, and connection in your interactions with others, leading to more effective communication and stronger relationships based on mutual respect.

Active Listening Techniques
Focus and Attention
Demonstrate genuine interest in the speaker by giving them your full and undivided attention (but don't stare them down; remember to blink). Minimise distractions and actively engage in the conversation by making eye contact, nodding and using appropriate (open and gentle vs defensive) body language to convey attentiveness and interest.

If this is an important conversation that may have significant repercussions, it is acceptable to make notes, let the speaker know you will be doing this to make sure you don't miss something important. If both parties agree, you may also consider recording a conversation,

Chapter 10: Effective Communication in Business and Life

or if on a platform like Zoom or Teams, use their transcription functions.

Reflective Responses

Paraphrase – offer them a brief summary of their key points to demonstrate understanding and validate their perspective. Reflective responses involve restating what the speaker has said in your own words, which shows that you are actively listening and processing their message. This is also a great way to make sure you have fully understood what they were saying and if not, it allows them to clarify. Paraphrasing is a powerful tool to avoid misunderstanding especially in important business-related communication.

Ask Clarifying Questions

Seek clarification to ensure accurate interpretation of the speaker's message. Asking clarifying questions helps to fill in any gaps in your understanding and allows the speaker to elaborate on their points. It also shows that you are genuinely interested in understanding their perspective.

Empathy and Validation

Acknowledge the speaker's emotions and experiences with empathy and validation. Validate their feelings by expressing understanding and empathy for their situation, even if you may not agree with their perspective. Empathic responses help to build trust and rapport, fostering a supportive and empathetic communication environment. Empathy and validation are essential communicational skills in every relationship which help people feel seen and heard and reassured that their opinions and thoughts are valued even if not everyone agrees with them.

Conflict Resolution Strategies
Mark Goulston's approach of Surgical Empathy, George Kohlrieser's research on Hostage Negotiation and Marshall Rosenberg's contribution to Non-Violent Communication have underscored the profound role of empathy in communication.

Goulston (2015), emphasised the importance of empathetic communication and listening in building trust and rapport with others, highlighting the significance of listening with the intent to understand, validate emotions and foster genuine connections. By employing empathetic communication techniques, individuals can strengthen relationships, diffuse conflicts, and achieve mutually beneficial outcomes.

Renowned psychologist and negotiation expert, George Kohlrieser's work focuses on the role of implementing hostage negotiation principles in business and personal communication. Like Goulston and Rosenberg, his research underscores the importance of building rapport, establishing trust and managing emotions in high-stakes interactions. By applying hostage negotiation strategies such as active listening, empathy and collaborative problem-solving, individuals can navigate challenging situations with confidence and achieve positive outcomes.

Chapter 10: Effective Communication in Business and Life

Rosenberg (2006) developed Nonviolent Communication (NVC) as a compassion-based communication tool whose aim is to foster compassionate connection and understanding between individuals, resolving conflicts peacefully and effectively. NVC encourages individuals to express themselves honestly, while also empathetically listening to others' feelings and needs.

The process involves four components: *observation*, *feelings*, *needs* and *requests*, which help individuals communicate in a way that avoids blame, judgment and hostility. Similarly, Goulston's emphasis on empathetic communication highlights the power of understanding and validating others' emotions to build trust and rapport.

The following case study demonstrates the application of surgical empathy, hostage negotiation principles and nonviolent communication (NVC) to resolving a conflict between co-workers.

Sarah and John work together on a project team. Recently, Sarah noticed that John has been consistently arriving late to team meetings. This has caused frustration for Sarah and other team members, as it disrupts the flow of discussions and delays progress on the project.

Observation

Sarah begins by describing the specific behaviour she observed without judgment or interpretation even though it has affected her and made her feel frustrated. She says, "John, I've noticed that in the past few weeks, you've been arriving late to our team meetings."

Feelings

Sarah then expresses her feelings about John's behaviour. She says, "When you come late, I feel frustrated (anger) because it disrupts our meeting schedule, and I'm concerned (anxious) about meeting our project deadlines."

Needs

Sarah articulates her underlying needs or values that are impacted by John's behaviour. She says, "I value punctuality and effective communication within our team. It's important for me that we respect each other's time and commitments."

Requests

Sarah makes a specific request for a change in behaviour, focusing on a positive action that can address the issue. She says, "Would you be willing to make an effort to arrive on time to our future meetings? This would help us stay on track and ensure everyone's contributions are valued."

John listens to Sarah's concerns and acknowledges the impact of his behaviour on the team. He explains that he has been dealing with personal issues that have affected his ability to manage his time effectively. John agrees to make a conscious effort to prioritise punctuality and communicate any potential delays in advance.

Through this exchange, Sarah and John engage in a constructive dialogue that respects each other's perspectives and needs. By using NVC principles, they are able to address the conflict collaboratively and find a mutually acceptable solution.

Chapter 10: Effective Communication in Business and Life

However, had Sarah practiced a more empathic and compassionate approach as a leader, she would have reached out to John *much* earlier and identified what was causing the lateness. This will have given her insight and the option to appropriately talk through the situation and help John address his lateness or explore making reasonable adjustments by moving meetings to a later slot that may have reduced the pressure for John and perhaps benefitted the whole team as a result. Likewise, if John was struggling, it was his responsibility to make Sarah aware so that they could explore mutually beneficial options.

In **Goulston's** approach, Sarah listens attentively to John's concerns, validating his perspective by acknowledging his frustrations and anxieties around his lateness. She empathetically communicates that she understands his viewpoint and expresses her willingness to collaborate and find a solution that addresses **both** of their concerns.

However, what if John felt dismissed or discounted by Sarah and the rest of the team? Kohlrieser offers in an intervention:

A heated disagreement arises between colleagues during the team meeting, threatening to escalate into a conflict.

Sarah being the team leader, intervenes by employing active listening techniques, empathetically acknowledging each person's perspective and validating their concerns. She encourages open dialogue and collaborative problem-solving, focusing on finding common ground and reaching a resolution that meets the team's objectives.

Nonviolent Communication, Empathy and Hostage Negotiation Principles can be applied to resolve most conflicts and improve communication in all settings. Research has supported the effectiveness of all the above approaches in various contexts, including conflict resolution, interpersonal relationships and organisational communication leading to improved emotional intelligence, conflict resolution skills, and relationship satisfaction.

This is a great example of how different elements of communication can be put into action however, it takes practice to become an effective communicator. Here are some further elements to keep in mind during discussions.

Calmness and Composure
Maintain emotional control and avoid escalating conflicts. Stay calm and composed, even in tense situations, to prevent emotions from clouding judgment and exacerbating the conflict. Take deep breaths and use relaxation techniques to manage stress and maintain a level-headed approach to conflict resolution. Using mindfulness, breathing techniques and NCV can significantly enhance the effectiveness of the discussion and contribute to the desired outcome.

Identify Core Issues
Identify the root causes of conflict to address underlying concerns effectively. It is imperative to focus on the issue rather than each other even when someone's choices and decisions have caused problems. Take the time to understand the underlying reasons behind the conflict,

Chapter 10: Effective Communication in Business and Life

such as differing values, needs, or perceptions.

Had Sarah taken time to find out what was going on for John to repeatedly make him late for the meetings, she would have been able to manage her frustration and understand where John was coming from including whether John's behaviour was a passive aggressive attempt to destabilise Sarah's authority within the group. By identifying the core issues and the reasons for choices, you can work towards finding mutually acceptable solutions that address the root causes of the conflict as well as begin to explore preventative measures.

Seek Common Ground

Explore areas of agreement and shared interests to facilitate resolution. Focus on finding common ground and areas of mutual benefit that can serve as a foundation for resolving the conflict. Emphasise shared goals and values to build rapport and create a sense of collaboration towards finding a resolution. Similarly, employing a Solution-Focused approach and discussing what steps to take should conflicts or disagreements arise is also a powerful step to take here ensuring both or all parties have access to a remedy to resolve future issues.

Collaborative Problem-Solving

Encourage open dialogue and brainstorming to generate mutually acceptable solutions. Engage all parties involved in the conflict in a collaborative problem-solving process. Encourage open communication, active listening, and creative brainstorming to explore different perspectives and generate innovative solutions that meet the needs of all stakeholders. This approach will offer insight into whether an individual is genuinely struggling with an issue or is purposely trying to derail the working relationship.

Unfortunately, malicious intent whether from jealousy, racism, homophobia, their own incompetence or inability to cope, can and does cause individuals to behave in unacceptable ways. Whilst modelling compassionate behaviour, it is important to be mindful and question whether or not some are indeed trying to sabotage your hard work or position. Such behaviour is prevalent in all strata of life, particularly in competitive fields of business.

Effective Communication
Foster transparent and respectful communication to prevent misunderstandings and resolve conflicts constructively. Create an environment where all parties feel comfortable and are safe in expressing their thoughts, feelings and concerns openly and honestly. Use active listening techniques, empathetic responses and clear communication to ensure that messages are understood and conflicts are resolved in a respectful and constructive manner.

By incorporating these active listening techniques and conflict resolution strategies into your interpersonal interactions, you can foster positive communication, build trust and rapport, and effectively resolve conflicts in both personal and professional settings.

Summary

In summary, effective communication skills are indispensable for success in both business and life. By honing verbal and nonverbal communication skills, practicing active listening including empathy and employing conflict resolution strategies individuals can enhance their interpersonal relationships, foster collaboration and drive business success. Moreover, drawing insights from experts like Rosenberg, Goulston and Kohlrieser can provide valuable perspectives and practical strategies for improving communication effectiveness.

Self Reflection Questions

1. Reflect on a recent communication challenge you encountered in your professional or personal life. How did you address it and what did you learn from the experience?
2. Identify one aspect of your verbal communication style that you would like to improve. What specific steps can you take to enhance this aspect of your communication?
3. Describe a conflict resolution scenario in which you successfully applied active listening techniques. What strategies were most effective in reaching a resolution?

Bibliography

1. Carnegie, D. (2009). How to Win Friends and Influence People. Simon & Schuster.

2. Chapman, G. D. (2015). The 5 Love Languages: The Secret to Love that Lasts. Northfield Publishing.
3. Covey, S. R. (2004). The 7 Habits of Highly Effective People: Powerful Lessons in Personal Change. Free Press.
4. Goulston, M. (2015). Just Listen: Discover the Secret to Getting Through to Absolutely Anyone. AMACOM.
5. Guerrero, L. K., et al. (2017). Nonverbal Communication in Close Relationships. Routledge.
6. Kohlrieser, G. (2006). Hostage at the Table: How Leaders Can Overcome Conflict, Influence Others, and Raise Performance. Jossey-Bass.
7. Joyce, A. S., Piper, W. E., & Ogrodniczuk, J. S. (2007). Therapeutic alliance and cohesion variables as predictors of outcome in short-term group psychotherapy. International Journal of Group Psychotherapy, 57(3), 269-296.
8. Riek, B. M., Mania, E. W., & Gaertner, S. L. (2006). Intergroup threat and outgroup attitudes: A meta-analytic review. Personality and Social Psychology Review, 10(4), 336-353.
9. Rosenberg, M. B. (2003). Nonviolent Communication: A Language of Compassion. Puddledancer Press.

Further Reading

1. Goleman, D. (2006). Emotional Intelligence: Why It Can Matter More Than IQ. Bantam Books.
2. Guerrero, L. K., et al. (2017). Nonverbal Communication in Close Relationships. Routledge.
3. Gottman, J. M., & Silver, N. (2015). The Seven Principles for Making Marriage Work. Harmony.
4. Patterson, K., Grenny, J., McMillan, R., & Switzler, A. (2011). Crucial Conversations: Tools for Talking When Stakes Are High. McGraw-Hill Education.
5. Pink, D. H. (2013). To Sell Is Human: The Surprising Truth About Moving Others. Riverhead Books.

Chapter 11: Cultivating Emotional Intelligence

Understanding Emotional Intelligence and Its Impact on Entrepreneurship and Leadership

In the realm of leadership and personal development, emotional intelligence (EI) stands as a cornerstone for success. The ability to understand and manage one's own emotions and emotional reactions, as well as those of others, is crucial in navigating various interpersonal dynamics and achieving goals in business. In this chapter, we delve into the essence of emotional intelligence, drawing from contemporary research, ancient texts, and wisdom to provide insights and techniques for its cultivation.

Emotional intelligence (EI) is an essential and necessary component of effective leadership, encompassing a multifaceted skill set that enables individuals to perceive, understand, manage and utilise emotions effectively. Salovey and Mayer's (1990) research found that EI plays a pivotal role in influencing decision-making, communication and relationship-building within personal and organisational contexts.

Salovey and Mayer (1990) defined emotional intelligence as 'the ability to perceive, understand, manage and use emotions effectively'. They outlined four key components of EI:

1. **Perception of Emotion**: The ability to accurately perceive and identify emotions in oneself and others.

2. **Understanding Emotion**: The capacity to comprehend the complex relationships between emotions and to recognise how emotions evolve over time.

3. **Management of Emotion**: The skill to regulate and control one's own emotions as well as to influence the emotions of others.

4. **Use of Emotion**: The ability to harness emotions to facilitate thinking, problem-solving and interpersonal interactions.

Salovey and Mayer found that emotional intelligence plays a crucial role in every aspect of life, including personal and professional relationships, success, and overall well-being. They proposed that emotional intelligence can be developed and enhanced through education and training. This has profound implications on business success for individuals who may not feel as emotionally literate as they would like.

Gross' (1998) research built on the findings of Salovey and Mayer and defined emotions as "adaptive behavioural and physiological response tendencies that are called forth directly by evolutionarily significant situations" These response tendencies were affected by how they were initially input and conditioned and what emotions the

Chapter 11: Cultivating Emotional Intelligence

individuals associated with them. (See also the fight or flight response discussed in Ch1)

Gross' research on emotion regulation provides valuable insights that can help entrepreneurs enhance their emotional intelligence (EI) in several ways:

Awareness

Gross' model highlights the importance of being aware of one's emotions and their impact on decision-making and behaviour. Entrepreneurs can use this awareness to recognise their emotional responses to different situations, enabling them to identify and regulate them effectively.

Antecedent-Focused Regulation

Gross identifies strategies such as *situation selection, modification, attention deployment* and *cognitive change* to regulate emotions before they fully develop.

1. **Situation Selection**: This strategy involves choosing which situations to enter or avoid based on their emotional impact (for example avoiding a difficult relation or colleague). Entrepreneurs can proactively select environments or situations that are conducive to positive emotions and aligned with their goals. For example, they may choose to attend networking events where they can connect with supportive peers or avoid situations that typically trigger stress or negative emotions. By exercising discretion in their choices, entrepreneurs can set themselves up for success and minimise the likelihood of experiencing distressing emotions.

2. **Situation Modification**: This strategy involves making changes to the environment or circumstances to alter their emotional impact. Entrepreneurs may modify their workspace, such as adding plants or artwork to create a more pleasant atmosphere, or rearrange their schedule to prioritise tasks that evoke positive emotions. By actively shaping their surroundings, entrepreneurs can cultivate an environment that fosters emotional well-being and enhances productivity whilst also aiming to achieve a work-life balance.

3. **Attention Deployment**: Attention deployment involves directing focus *towards* or *away* from specific stimuli to influence one's emotions. Entrepreneurs can, with practice, deliberately shift their attention towards positive aspects of a situation, such as opportunities for growth or achievements, while diverting attention away from potential stressors or setbacks including employing strategies discussed throughout this book to address and overcome the stressors. Techniques like mindfulness meditation can help entrepreneurs cultivate greater awareness of their thoughts and emotions, allowing them to consciously redirect, reframe and reposition their attention towards more constructive and uplifting areas of focus.

4. **Cognitive Change**: Cognitive change involves reframing one's interpretation or appraisal of a situation to alter its emotional impact. Entrepreneurs can challenge and restructure their

negative or distorted thoughts, replacing them with more balanced and adaptive perspectives. For instance, instead of viewing a setback as a failure, entrepreneurs can reframe it as a learning opportunity or a temporary obstacle on the path to success. By harnessing the power of cognitive restructuring, entrepreneurs can transform their emotional responses and cultivate a resilient mindset that enables them to navigate challenges with greater ease and optimism.

By employing these antecedent-focused emotion regulation strategies, entrepreneurs can proactively manage their emotions, create conducive environments for success, and cultivate a resilient and adaptive mindset essential for thriving in the dynamic and unpredictable world of entrepreneurship.

Response-focused Regulation
Entrepreneurs often encounter unexpected setbacks and challenges that evoke strong emotional reactions which may also connect to present coping mechanisms. Gross' model suggests response-focused emotion regulation techniques like *intensifying, diminishing, prolonging,* or *curtailing* emotions after they arise can have a significant influence on the impact of the reaction *after* an emotional response has already been triggered. For example:

1. **Intensifying**: This technique involves deliberately amplifying an emotional experience. For example, an entrepreneur might intentionally intensify feelings of enthusiasm or passion to motivate

themselves or others, especially during challenging times or when seeking to inspire their team.

2. **Diminishing:** Conversely, diminishing emotions entails reducing the intensity of emotional experiences. Entrepreneurs may use this technique to mitigate feelings of anxiety, stress, or anger that could hinder their decision-making or interactions with others. For instance, they might employ relaxation techniques, such as deep breathing or mindfulness, to calm themselves down while also visualising the situation in context of their whole lives to gain perspective.

3. **Prolonging**: Prolonging emotions involves extending the duration of a particular emotional state. For instance, an entrepreneur may seek to prolong feelings of satisfaction or accomplishment after achieving a significant milestone in their business. By savouring (and celebrating) positive emotions, they can reinforce their motivation and resilience, which can be beneficial for long-term success.

4. **Curtailing**: Curtailing emotions refers to shortening the duration of an emotional experience. Entrepreneurs may use this technique to quickly recover from setbacks or negative experiences and regain focus on their goals. For example, when the carefully prepared PowerPoint presentation fails in front of a room of leaders, there is no time to panic! At this point they can call upon self-soothing

strategies and refocus their energy on what NEEDS to be done to salvage the situation. They might engage in self-soothing activities such as EFT using 'all is well' as a script to tap with, or cognitive reappraisal with or without support from a friend or mentor later to reduce the lingering effects of disappointment or frustration.

By employing these response-focused emotion regulation techniques, entrepreneurs can exert greater control over their emotional experiences, effectively managing their reactions to various situations and optimizing their performance in the dynamic and demanding world of entrepreneurship.

Cognitive Reappraisal Techniques
Cognitive reappraisal involves reframing negative thoughts and emotions in a more positive or constructive light. Gross and John (2003) demonstrated that cognitive reappraisal strategies can effectively modulate emotional responses and promote psychological well-being. By shifting one's perspective and focusing on alternative interpretations of a situation, individuals can reduce the intensity of negative emotions and maintain perspective in challenging circumstances.

Cognitive reappraisal techniques can be practiced by consciously challenging and reframing negative thoughts as they arise. For example, if facing a setback at work, instead of catastrophising the situation ('This is an *absolute* disaster!'), reframe it as a learning opportunity ('What can I learn from this experience?').

Organisational Context: Gross' model acknowledges the influence of the environment on emotional experiences. Entrepreneurs can apply these insights to foster a supportive and emotionally intelligent culture within their networking groups, peer support circles and organisations, where employees are encouraged to regulate their emotions effectively, leading to better collaboration, communication and productivity.

Continuous Learning and Adaptation
Gross' model also emphasises that emotion regulation is a dynamic process that requires ongoing learning and adaptation. Entrepreneurs can cultivate a growth mindset towards emotional intelligence, continually seeking feedback from self-reflection as well as from trusted others, experimenting with different strategies and refining their approach based on outcomes.

In Japan, where teamwork and interpersonal harmony are deeply ingrained cultural values, the role of emotional intelligence (EI) in fostering effective communication and collaboration cannot be overstated.

Yamaguchi et al. (2019) highlighted the critical importance of EI in navigating the nuances of interpersonal relationships within Japanese workplaces. Employees who possess higher levels of EI demonstrate a remarkable ability to adapt to diverse interpersonal dynamics, thereby enhancing overall team cohesion, productivity and a sense of harmony from reduced discord and friction (Matsui & Kakuyama, 2017). This adaptability enables them to navigate through intricate social hierarchies and cultural norms, facilitating smoother interactions and more efficient teamwork.

Furthermore, organisations in Japan that prioritise EI training and development initiatives have been found to enjoy additional tangible benefits. Sato and Saito (2020) found that such organisations experience lower turnover rates and higher levels of employee satisfaction. By investing in the emotional intelligence of their workforce, these organisations create a more supportive and harmonious work environment, ultimately contributing to enhanced employee well-being and organisational success.

Similarly, in cultures renowned for their cohesive workplace environments, such as those found in Scandinavia, emotional intelligence plays a pivotal role in shaping effective leadership and team dynamics. Andersen and Hansen (2018) emphasise that leaders with high EI possess essential qualities such as empathy, self-awareness and conflict management skills.

These leaders are adept at understanding and responding to the emotional needs of their team members, fostering a sense of psychological safety and trust within the workplace. This supportive environment encourages innovation, collaboration and open communication, thus adding to the sense of psychological safety ultimately driving organisational success (Gundersen et al., 2016).

Implementing findings from Japanese studies on emotional intelligence requires a holistic approach that integrates cultural sensitivity, interpersonal skills development, and organisational leadership practices.

Organisations can adopt various strategies to cultivate emotional intelligence among their leaders and teams, including:

Cultural Sensitivity Training
Providing leaders with training and resources to develop cultural competence and sensitivity to the unique dynamics of Japanese and Scandinavian workplaces can significantly help to enhance their own leadership style. This may include workshops, cross-cultural immersion experiences and ongoing coaching with a culturally competent and aware Coach to enhance cultural awareness and adaptability.

The Japanese concept of 'wa,' meaning harmony or unity, offers valuable insights into fostering emotional balance and mutual respect within teams. Takano and Osaka (1999) explored the cultural roots of 'wa' in Japanese society and its implications for organisational dynamics.

By promoting open communication, embracing diversity and differences in perspectives and fostering a culture of mutual respect, leaders can create an atmosphere of emotional harmony that enhances team cohesion and performance, reduces friction, stress and positively impacts the level of sickness absence and productivity. You can foster a culture of '**wa**' within your team by promoting open dialogue, active listening and respectful constructive feedback. Encourage team members to express their thoughts and feelings openly, creating a safe space for honest communication and collaboration. Embrace diversity of perspectives and seek input from individuals with varied backgrounds and experiences, harnessing the collective wisdom and creativity of your team towards shared goals.

Interpersonal Skills Development

Offering training programs focused on enhancing key interpersonal skills such as empathy, active listening, and conflict resolution enable leaders to gain invaluable experience and insight. These programs can provide leaders with practical tools and techniques for building rapport, fostering trust, and promoting effective communication within multicultural teams.

Leadership Development Initiatives

Implementing leadership development initiatives that prioritise emotional intelligence as a core competency for success offer great value. This may involve incorporating EI assessments into leadership assessments, providing targeted coaching and feedback and creating opportunities for leaders to practice and refine their emotional intelligence skills in real-world scenarios.

Organisational Culture Transformation

Fostering a culture that values emotional intelligence, collaboration, and diversity of perspectives is invaluable to organisations. Leaders can model EI behaviours, establish clear expectations for respectful communication and interpersonal conduct, and reward individuals and teams that demonstrate high levels of emotional intelligence in their work.

Understanding the impact of emotional intelligence on leadership effectiveness requires a nuanced exploration of cultural context, interpersonal dynamics and organisational practices. By leveraging insights from research findings, particularly from studies conducted in Japan, organisations can cultivate emotional intelligence among their leaders and teams, leading to enhanced collaboration, innovation and ultimately, success in today's global marketplace.

Enhancing Emotional Regulation Skills

Emotional regulation is vital for effective leadership, enabling individuals to manage their emotions adaptively and maintain composure in challenging situations. Recent research has underscored the importance of emotional regulation in leadership effectiveness, highlighting its role in fostering resilience, reducing stress, and promoting positive workplace outcomes.

Summary

In this section, we explored techniques for enhancing emotional intelligence and emotional regulation skills, drawing upon contemporary research findings and practical implementation strategies. Entrepreneurs can apply these and other strategies offered by Gross, Salovey and Mayer's work amongst others, by carefully choosing the environments they operate in, modifying their workspaces to promote positive emotions, directing their

Chapter 11: Cultivating Emotional Intelligence

attention towards constructive aspects of their business, and reframing their perspectives on challenges.

Enhancing emotional regulation skills is essential for effective leadership and organisational success. By incorporating cognitive reappraisal techniques and drawing inspiration from cultural concepts such as 'wa,' leaders can cultivate emotional balance, foster positive workplace dynamics, and empower their teams to thrive in today's complex and dynamic environment.

Whether in Japan, Scandinavia or any country in the world, the importance of emotional intelligence in promoting effective communication, collaboration, and leadership cannot be understated. Cultivating EI within the workforce not only enhances individual and team performance but also contributes to a more positive and cohesive organisational culture.

Self-Reflection Questions:
1. Reflect on a recent challenging situation where you experienced strong emotions. How did you respond emotionally, and how did this impact your thoughts, behaviours and interactions with others? Reflect on what insights you gained from this experience about your own emotional reactions and coping mechanisms.
2. Choose one aspect of emotional intelligence discussed in the chapter that you feel could benefit from further development for you. This could be self-awareness, empathy, emotional regulation, or fostering emotional balance within teams. Outline

specific strategies and action steps you will implement to cultivate this skill in your daily life and professional interactions.
3. Identify a leader, either within your organisation or in the public domain, whom you admire for their demonstrated emotional intelligence. What specific qualities, behaviours, or practices do they exhibit that contribute to their effectiveness as a leader? Reflect on how you can incorporate these attributes into your own leadership style and interactions with others.
4. Reflect on the concept of 'wa' or harmony discussed in the chapter. How can you promote a culture of emotional balance, mutual respect and collaboration within your team or organisation? Consider practical steps you can take to foster open communication, embrace diversity of perspectives and create a supportive work environment where individuals feel valued and empowered.

Bibliography:
1. Batson, C. D., et al. (1995). 'Is empathy-induced helping due to self-other merging? Journal of Personality and Social Psychology, 68(3), 387–396.
2. Gross, J. J., & John, O. P. (2003). Individual differences in two emotion regulation processes: Implications for affect, relationships, and well-being. Journal of Personality and Social Psychology, 85(2), 348–362.
3. Kabat-Zinn, J., et al. (2013). Mindfulness-based stress reduction for health care professionals: Results from a randomized trial. International Journal of Stress Management, 20(2), 164–176
4. Matsui, T., & Kakuyama, T. (2017). Influence of emotional intelligence on team performance through the mediation of communication: Toward the realization of workplace reform. The Japanese Journal of Psychology, 88(3), 283–292. https://doi.org/10.4992/jjpsy.88.16151

5. Salovey, P., & Mayer, J. D. (1990). Emotional intelligence. Imagination, Cognition, and Personality, 9(3), 185-211.
6. Sato, Y., & Saito, E. (2020). The relationship between emotional intelligence, social support, and turnover intention among Japanese nurses. Nursing & Health Sciences, 22(4), 985–992. https://doi.org/10.1111/nhs.12733
7. Takano, Y., & Osaka, E. (1999). An unsupported common view: Comparing Japan and the U.S. on individualism/collectivism. Asian Journal of Social Psychology, 2(3), 311–341.
8. Yamaguchi, A., Katsura, T., & Okumura, T. (2019). Influence of emotional intelligence on organizational commitment and job satisfaction: The case of Japanese nurses. Japan Journal of Nursing Science, 16(1), 38–47. https://doi.org/10.1111/jjns.12217

Further Reading:

1. Brackett, M. A. (2019). Permission to Feel: Unlocking the Power of Emotions to Help Our Kids, Ourselves, and Our Society Thrive. Celadon Books.
2. Goleman, D. (2009). Emotional Intelligence: Why It Can Matter More Than IQ. Bloomsbury Publishing.
3. Hanh, T. N. (2016). The Miracle of Mindfulness: An Introduction to the Practice of Meditation. Beacon Press.
4. Hofstede, G., et al. (2010). Cultures and Organisations: Software of the Mind. McGraw-Hill Education.
5. Krishna, Bhagavad Gita. Translated by Eknath Easwaran, Nilgiri Press, 2007.
6. Matsumoto, D. (2020). The Handbook of Culture and Psychology. Oxford University Press.
7. Suzuki, D. T. (2011). Zen Mind, Beginner's Mind. Shambhala Publications.

Chapter 12: Harnessing the Power of Gratitude

What Ancient Tribal Practices Can Teach Us

Gratitude, often described as the practice of recognising and appreciating the good in one's life, has garnered increasing attention in psychological research due to its profound impact on mental health and overall well-being. From reducing stress and depression to improving both personal and professional relationships whilst enhancing overall life satisfaction, the benefits of gratitude are far-reaching and well-documented.

Gratitude is not only a phenomenon observed in modern societies but has also been a fundamental aspect of traditional tribal cultures around the world. These cultures offer valuable insights into the innate human inclination towards gratitude and its profound impact on mental health and well-being. Let's explore some examples from tribal studies.

Indigenous Cultures of North America

Many Indigenous tribes in North America, such as the Navajo, Cherokee, Sioux and Lakota, have rich traditions of gratitude deeply intertwined with their spiritual beliefs and daily practices. For instance, the Navajo practice of **'be'eldíí'** or **'be'eldǫǫdaa'** involves expressing gratitude for the interconnectedness of all living beings and the natural world. Tribes often hold ceremonies, such as the 'Giveaway' or 'Potlatch,' where individuals express gratitude by giving away possessions or sharing resources with others. These practices not only foster a sense of community and reciprocity but also contribute to overall well-being by promoting gratitude and generosity.

Maori Culture of New Zealand

The Maori people of New Zealand have a concept known as **'whakawhanaungatanga**,' which emphasises the importance of building and maintaining relationships based on mutual respect and gratitude. Gratitude is expressed through rituals such as the **'hongi**,' a traditional greeting where individuals press their foreheads and noses together, symbolising the sharing of breath and acknowledging each other's presence. Additionally, the Maori tradition of **'koha**,' or gift-giving, is rooted in gratitude and reciprocity, strengthening social bonds and promoting a sense of belonging within the community.

Aboriginal Cultures of Australia

Aboriginal cultures in Australia have long embraced gratitude as a core value essential for maintaining harmony with the land and each other. Practices such as **'Dadirri**,' meaning deep listening and inner stillness, encourage individuals to cultivate gratitude by connecting with the natural world and appreciating its beauty and wisdom. Aboriginal ceremonies, such as **'Welcome to Country'** and **'Smoking Ceremony**,' acknowledge the ancestral spirits and express gratitude for their guidance and protection.

African Tribal Communities

Across various African tribal communities, gratitude is woven into everyday life through rituals, ceremonies and communal celebrations. For example, the '**Ubuntu**' philosophy of power in unity prevalent in many African cultures emphasises the interconnectedness of humanity and the importance of expressing gratitude cohesion and compassion towards others.

In Nigeria, the Yoruba people practice '**Ire**,' a concept encompassing blessings, good fortune and gratitude for life's abundance. Through song, dance and storytelling, African tribes express gratitude for the land, ancestors and community, fostering a sense of belonging and resilience in the face of adversity.

In each of these tribal cultures, gratitude is not merely a fleeting emotion but a way of life deeply embedded in cultural practices, rituals, and belief systems passed down through millennia. By honouring the interconnectedness of all beings, expressing appreciation for the gifts of nature and fostering a spirit of generosity and reciprocity, tribal communities around the world exemplify the transformative power of gratitude in promoting mental health, well-being and harmony with the world around us. These examples underscore the universal relevance of gratitude across diverse cultural contexts and highlight its enduring significance for human flourishing.

Research has consistently demonstrated the profound impact of gratitude on mental health and well-being, encompassing various dimensions of human experience. Let's delve deeper into these benefits with practical examples:

Improved Psychological Health

Consider Sarah, a young professional struggling with feelings of stress and dissatisfaction in her life. After learning about the concept of gratitude, she decides to incorporate a daily gratitude journalling practice into her routine. Each evening, Sarah reflects on three things she's grateful for, whether it's the support of her friends, the beauty of nature during her morning walk, or the small victories at work. Over time, Sarah notices a significant shift in her mood and outlook on life. She feels more content, resilient in the face of challenges, and experiences fewer symptoms of depression and anxiety. This transformation echoes findings from Wood et al., (2010), who reported significant improvements in overall psychological well-being among individuals who participated in gratitude interventions compared to those who did not.

Enhanced Relationships

Imagine Johaan and Maria, a couple navigating the complexities of their relationship. Recognising the importance of expressing gratitude, they decide to incorporate daily gratitude rituals into their lives. Each evening, they take turns expressing appreciation for each other's efforts, whether it's a thoughtful gesture or a simple act of kindness.

Through this practice, Johaan and Maria deepen their emotional connection, strengthen their bond, and experience greater relationship satisfaction. This echoes research by Algoe et al. (2013), which suggests that expressing gratitude towards a romantic partner leads to increased relationship satisfaction and deeper emotional bonds.

Physical Health Benefits
Picture Mark, a middle-aged professional struggling to maintain a healthy lifestyle due to the demands of his job. Inspired by research linking gratitude to physical health benefits, he decides to incorporate gratitude practices into his daily routine. Each morning, Mark starts his day by expressing gratitude for his body's strength and vitality, setting a positive tone for the day ahead. Over time, this small practice inspired and motivated Mark to make better health choices in the foods he ate and in his self-care behaviours. Mark noticed improvements in his sleep quality, energy levels, and overall physical well-being. Hill et al. (2013), found that gratitude was positively associated with better sleep quality, contributing to overall physical health.

Resilience and Coping Skills
Think of Emily, a student facing academic challenges and personal setbacks. Determined to build resilience, she begins practising gratitude as a way to reframe her mindset during difficult times. Whenever Emily encounters obstacles, she takes a moment to reflect on her feelings, learning to make space for them and what lessons she might take away from the experiences. She also focuses on

the things she's grateful for, such as supportive friends or moments of joy in her day. Through this practice, Emily cultivates a sense of resilience, enabling her to navigate setbacks with grace and optimism.

Emmons and McCullough (2003), revealed that individuals who regularly engage in gratitude exercises are better equipped to cope with stress and adversity. By integrating gratitude practices into their daily lives, individuals like Sarah, Johaan, Maria, Mark, and Emily can unlock the transformative power of gratitude, experiencing tangible improvements in their mental, emotional, and physical well-being. These examples underscore the real-world applicability of research-backed benefits and highlight the profound impact of gratitude on human flourishing.

Practices for Cultivating Gratitude in Daily Life
Gratitude Journalling
Keeping a gratitude journal involves regularly writing down things you are thankful for. This practice encourages mindfulness and helps shift focus towards positive aspects of life. To implement this, set aside a few minutes each day to reflect on three things you are grateful for and jot them down in a journal.

Each evening, take a moment to reflect on the events of the day and before bed identify three moments or experiences that brought you joy or gratitude. Write them down in your journal, focusing on the specific details that made them meaningful to you. The more details you are able to go into, the deeper your understanding of the vastness of the event that you are contemplating. For example, giving thanks for a meal could make you think of having the food and the facilities to prepare it. The money to buy the food and pay for the facilities to cook it i.e. a kitchen in a home. Expand that to a cooker and fridge in the kitchen. Now go deeper, who made the cooker and fridge, and deeper still, the people that made the components, and deeper still, the miners who dug up the ores to make metals. Similarly the food you are preparing, the carrot's journey from seed to plant to harvest to the supermarket, to your plate. We forget the many steps and people who are vital to our being able to do the most basic things. You can also add what you are looking forward to on the following day.

Gratitude Letter Writing
Composing a gratitude letter involves expressing appreciation to someone (including yourself!) who has positively impacted your life. Seligman et al. (2005) suggests that both writing and delivering such letters can significantly increase happiness and well-being, not only form that physical act of doing so, but also from the (hopefully) effervescent response from the recipient.

Think of someone who has made a significant difference in your life, whether it's a family member, friend, mentor or even a shop assistant. Write a heartfelt letter expressing your gratitude, detailing how their actions have influenced you and why you are thankful for their presence in your life.

Mindful Gratitude Practice

Engaging in mindful gratitude involves being fully present and attentive to experiences of gratitude as they arise throughout the day. This practice encourages awareness of the abundance of blessings in one's life, no matter how small.

Throughout the day, pause for a moment whenever you experience a feeling of gratitude, whether it's enjoying a warm cup of tea, witnessing a beautiful sunset, or receiving a kind gesture from a someone. Take a deep breath, savour the moment, and express gratitude for the experience.

Gratitude Practices Around the World

Gratitude is a universal concept, yet its expression varies across cultures.

Japanese Tradition of O-kyuji

In Japan, the practice of **O-kyuji** involves expressing gratitude before meals. This tradition acknowledges the efforts of those involved in preparing the food and the interconnectedness of all beings from the farmer to the person who prepared the food, to the person who made the dinnerware, etc.

South African Concept of Ubuntu

Ubuntu, meaning 'I am because we are,' emphasises the importance of gratitude and interconnectedness within communities. Expressing gratitude and appreciation for others is integral to this philosophy and to survival. Remember Dave our hunter-gatherer, I imagine there was a great deal of gratitude amongst his tribe for surviving another day and having food to eat.

Native American Thanksgiving Rituals
Many Native American cultures have traditions of giving thanks to nature, ancestors, and the spirit world through ceremonies and rituals that honour the interconnectedness of all living beings.

Hawaiian Tradition of Ho'oponopono
Ho'oponopono is a Hawaiian practice of reconciliation and forgiveness that involves expressing gratitude and seeking harmony with oneself and others through prayer and meditation. There is a mantra that helps individuals overcome negative experiences and hurt from others:

I love you (regardless of what you have done to me, because I choose to offer only love)
I am sorry (for any slight or wrong I may have done you)
Please forgive me (if I have hurt you in any way)
Thank you (I receive and acknowledge your forgiveness whether you choose to give it or not)

Indian Tradition of Pranāma
In India, the practice of **Pranāma** involves expressing gratitude and respect by bowing or touching the feet of elders, teachers and spiritual leaders. This gesture acknowledges their wisdom, guidance, and contributions to one's life journey. Pranāma reflects the belief in the interconnectedness of generations and the importance of honouring those who have paved the way.

Thai Custom of Wai
In Thailand, the **Wai** (or Namaste) is a traditional greeting and gesture of respect that also embodies gratitude. By pressing their palms together in a prayer-like gesture and

bowing slightly, individuals express gratitude and reverence towards others, whether they are family members, friends, or strangers. The Wai reflects the Thai cultural values of humility, gratitude, and mutual respect.

Irish Tradition of Saying 'Thank You' with a Blessing

In Ireland, gratitude is often expressed through the art of storytelling and blessing. When someone offers a kind gesture or assistance, it is customary to respond with a heartfelt 'thank you' accompanied by a blessing such as 'God bless you' or 'May the road rise to meet you.' This tradition not only acknowledges the kindness received but also extends blessings and good wishes to the giver, fostering a sense of connection and goodwill within the community.

Tibetan Practice of Offering Khata

In Tibetan culture, the **Khata** is a ceremonial scarf offered as a symbol of respect, gratitude and well-wishing. When visiting temples, monasteries, or homes of elders, individuals present Khata to express gratitude and seek blessings for auspicious occasions or significant life events. This gesture embodies the spirit of gratitude and reverence for spiritual teachings, community elders, and cherished relationships.

Moroccan Tradition of Hospitality and Gift-Giving

In Morocco, gratitude is often expressed through acts of hospitality and gift-giving. When visiting someone's home, it is customary to bring a small gift such as flowers, sweets, or pastries as a token of appreciation. Similarly, hosts go to great lengths to ensure their guests feel

Chapter 12: Harnessing the Power of Gratitude

welcomed and cared for, expressing gratitude for their presence through generous hospitality and warm gestures including food and gifts in return.

Inuit Tradition of Gift Exchange

Among the Inuit people of the Arctic regions, gratitude is deeply intertwined with the practice of gift exchange known as **'Potlatch'** or **'Nalukataq.'** During these ceremonial gatherings, individuals give and receive gifts such as food, clothing, tools and handicrafts as a way of expressing gratitude, honouring relationships, and strengthening social bonds within the community. The act of giving is seen as a reciprocal gesture, fostering generosity, solidarity, and mutual support. In ancient times, such gift would have been associated with survival and fostering a sense of community in harsh environments.

Summary

These examples highlight the richness and diversity of gratitude practices found across cultures, each reflecting unique values, beliefs, and traditions. These practices not only foster a sense of belonging and interconnectedness but also promote mental and emotional well-being by grounding individuals in gratitude and respect for their cultural heritage.

Whether through gestures of respect, acts of hospitality, or ceremonial rituals, expressions of gratitude serve to deepen connections, foster reciprocity, and cultivate a sense of belonging and harmony within communities around the world.

Self Reflection Questions
1. Reflect on a recent experience that elicited feelings of gratitude. How did acknowledging and expressing gratitude for this experience impact your mood and perspective?
2. Choose one gratitude practice discussed in this chapter (e.g., gratitude journalling, letter writing) and commit to incorporating it into your daily routine for the next week. What insights or changes do you notice in your mindset and well-being as a result?
3. Explore a gratitude practice from a culture different from your own (e.g., Japanese O-kyuji, South African Ubuntu). How does this practice resonate with you, and how might you incorporate elements of it into your own gratitude rituals?
4. Think of a person in your life whom you appreciate but have not expressed gratitude towards recently. How can you show them appreciation and gratitude in a meaningful way?

Bibliography
1. Algoe, S. B., Gable, S. L., & Maisel, N. C. (2010). It's the little things: Everyday gratitude as a booster shot for romantic relationships. Personal Relationships, 17(2), 217-233.
2. Emmons, R. A., & McCullough, M. E. (2003). Counting blessings versus burdens: An experimental investigation of gratitude and subjective well-being in daily life. Journal of Personality and Social Psychology, 84(2), 377–389.
3. Froh, J. J., Emmons, R. A., Card, N. A., Bono, G., & Wilson, J. A. (2011). Gratitude and the reduced costs of materialism in adolescents. Journal of Happiness Studies, 12(2), 289–302.
4. Hill, P. L., Allemand, M., & Roberts, B. W. (2013). Examining the pathways between gratitude and self-rated physical health across adulthood. Personality and Individual Differences, 54(1), 92–96.

5. Hill, P. L., Allemand, M., Roberts, B. W., & Johnson, S. K. (2013). Positive and negative affective instability in daily life: Associations with well-being and sleep. Personality and Individual Differences, 54(7), 902–907.
6. Kashdan, T. B., Mishra, A., Breen, W. E., & Froh, J. J. (2009). Gender differences in gratitude: Examining appraisals, narratives, the willingness to express emotions, and changes in psychological needs. Journal of Personality, 77(3), 691–730.
7. McCullough, M. E., Emmons, R. A., & Tsang, J. (2002). The grateful disposition: A conceptual and empirical topography. Journal of Personality and Social Psychology, 82(1), 112–127.
8. McCullough, M. E., Kilpatrick, S. D., Emmons, R. A., & Larson, D. B. (2001). Is gratitude a moral affect? Psychological Bulletin, 127(2), 249–266.
9. Rash, J. A., Matsuba, M. K., & Prkachin, K. M. (2011). Gratitude and well-being: Who benefits the most from a gratitude intervention? Applied Psychology: Health and Well-Being, 3(3), 350–369.
10. Sansone, R. A., & Sansone, L. A. (2010). Gratitude and well-being: the benefits of appreciation. Psychiatry (Edgmont), 7(11), 18–22.
11. Seligman, M. E., Steen, T. A., Park, N., & Peterson, C. (2005). Positive psychology progress: Empirical validation of interventions. American Psychologist, 60(5), 410–421.
12. Sin, N. L., & Lyubomirsky, S. (2009). Enhancing well-being and alleviating depressive symptoms with positive psychology interventions: A practice-friendly meta-analysis. Journal of Clinical Psychology, 65(5), 467–487.
13. Wood, A. M., Froh, J. J., & Geraghty, A. W. A. (2010). Gratitude and well-being: A review and theoretical integration. Clinical Psychology Review, 30(7), 890–905.
14. Wood, A. M., Joseph, S., & Maltby, J. (2009). Gratitude predicts psychological well-being above the Big Five facets. Personality and Individual Differences, 46(4), 443–447.

Further Reading

1. Amin, A., & Froh, J. J. (Eds.). (2020). Positive Psychology in Practice: Promoting Human Flourishing in Work, Health, Education, and Everyday Life. John Wiley & Sons.
2. Donohue, J. O. (2004). Beauty: The Invisible Embrace. Harper Perennial.
3. Fredrickson, B. L. (2009). Positivity: Groundbreaking Research Reveals How to Embrace the Hidden Strength of Positive Emotions, Overcome Negativity, and Thrive. Crown Publishing Group.

4. Froh, J. J., & Bono, G. (2014). Making Grateful Kids: The Science of Building Character. Templeton Press.
5. Keltner, D., & Marsh, J. (2018). The Power Paradox: How We Gain and Lose Influence. Penguin Random House.
6. Korb, A. (2015). The Upward Spiral: Using Neuroscience to Reverse the Course of Depression, One Small Change at a Time. New Harbinger Publications.
7. Lyubomirsky, S. (2007). The How of Happiness: A Scientific Approach to Getting the Life You Want. Penguin Books.
8. Lyubomirsky, S. (2008). The How of Happiness: A Scientific Approach to Getting the Life You Want. Penguin Books.
9. Seligman, M. E. (2011). Flourish: A Visionary New Understanding of Happiness and Well-being. Simon & Schuster.
10. Snyder, C. R., & Lopez, S. J. (Eds.). (2002). Handbook of Positive Psychology. Oxford University Press.
11. Tagore, R. (1997). The Gardener. Rupa & Co.
12. Vaillant, G. E. (2008). Aging Well: Surprising Guideposts to a Happier Life from the Landmark Harvard Study of Adult Development. Little, Brown and Company.
13. Watkins, P. C. (2014). Gratitude and the Good Life: Toward a Psychology of Appreciation. Springer Science & Business Media.
14. Wong, J., & Brown, J. (2017). The Science of Gratitude: How It Improves Your Health, Happiness, and Relationships. Zephyros Press.
15. Wong, P. T. (2012). The Human Quest for Meaning: Theories, Research, and Applications. Routledge.

Chapter 13: Resilience in Entrepreneurship: A Vital Skill for Success

Building a Resilient Mindset

In today's dynamic and ever-changing landscape of the entrepreneurial world, the ability and capacity to adapt and bounce back from setbacks amidst adversities and challenges is more important than ever. Developing a resilient mindset is not only crucial for navigating life's ups and downs but also for thriving in the face of all the adversities that are linked to being an entrepreneur. Resilience stands as a crucial attribute in determining success or failure.

In this chapter, we will explore the characteristics of a resilient mindset, techniques for building mental toughness and adaptability, strategies for reframing challenges in entrepreneurship, its significance, strategies to cultivate it effectively, and openly discuss the detrimental effects of toxic resilience on mental health and well-being.

Understanding the Characteristics of a Resilient Mindset

Resilience, in the entrepreneurial context, refers to the ability to bounce back from setbacks, adapt to change, maintain focus and determination in pursuing business goals (Smith & Woodworth, 2012). It encompasses emotional, cognitive and behavioural facets, enabling entrepreneurs to navigate uncertainties and persevere in the face of failures and obstacles.

Significance of Resilience

Research suggests a strong correlation between resilience and entrepreneurial success. Entrepreneurs with high levels of resilience demonstrate greater persistence, creativity, and problem-solving skills, essential for sustaining ventures in volatile markets (Ratten, 2017). Likewise, resilient entrepreneurs exhibit improved mental well-being and reduced stress levels, enhancing overall performance and decision-making (Baron, 2008).

Factors Influencing Resilience

Several factors contribute to the development of resilience among entrepreneurs. Personal traits such as optimism or having a 'glass half-full' attitude, self-efficacy, and locus of control (what a person believes about who or what has the control over their lives), play pivotal roles in fostering resilience (Chen et al., 2018). Additionally, social support networks which dilute or diminish feelings of isolation and loneliness, access to resources and prior experiences of overcoming challenges significantly influence an entrepreneur's resilience quotient (Frese & Gielnik, 2014). Similarly, how someone perceives hurdles and barriers in relations to their previous experiences also has a significant impact on an individual's capacity for emotional buoyancy and recovery from setbacks and disappointments such as those proposed by Gross (1998, 2003) in Ch 11.

Cultivating Resilience

Entrepreneurs can actively cultivate resilience through various strategies. These include acknowledging and embracing failure as a highly valuable and powerful learning opportunity in the long term (see **Ch 9**). Additionally, as has been suggested in previous chapters, practicing mindfulness and stress management techniques, setting realistic goals, and seeking mentorship and peer support have beneficial outcomes for entrepreneurs (Rauch & Hulsink, 2015).

Additionally, maintaining a sense of purpose even after experiencing a setback (not everything has to be seen as a failure), and exercising adaptability, along with effective problem-solving skills, strengthens an entrepreneur's resilience arsenal (Cardon et al., 2017).

Toxic Resilience and Its Impact on Mental Health

While resilience is generally regarded as beneficial, there exists a phenomenon known as toxic resilience, wherein individuals suppress emotions, ignore their well-being, and persist in unhealthy patterns despite mounting stressors (Sood, 2016). In the entrepreneurial context, toxic resilience may manifest as a relentless pursuit of success at the expense of personal health, strained relationships and ethical compromises.

Entrepreneurs exhibiting toxic resilience may experience heightened levels of chronic stress, anxiety, and burnout (Luthar et al., 2000). The relentless pressure to succeed coupled with inadequate coping mechanisms, further exacerbated by internalised cultural narratives around failure leading to feelings of shame can lead to emotional exhaustion, decreased productivity, and impaired decision-making abilities.

Burnout as a Badge of Honour

In both Japanese and Chinese cultures, there exists a strong emphasis on diligence, perseverance, and maintaining harmony within society (Smith, 2008; Wu & Tseng, 2016). Consequently, burnout, anxiety and struggling to cope are often frowned upon, albeit in somewhat different ways. In executives collapsing from exhaustion, toxic resilience is seen as a badge of honour and preferable compared to the disdain with which admitting to feelings of fatigue, anxiety or depression are viewed.

This concept is known as "**karoshi**" (death by overwork) in Japanese culture, and highlights the severe consequences of burnout and excessive work-related stress (Kivimaki et al., 2011). Despite the prevalence of long working hours and intense pressure in many Japanese companies, openly acknowledging mental health struggles or seeking help for burnout is often stigmatised (Suzuki, 2018). There is a societal expectation to endure hardship without complaint and prioritise dedication to one's work and responsibilities (Tanaka, 2019). Veering from the norm results in deep distress and ostracisation from society not only for the individual concerned, but the whole family, including children who are stigmatised and shunned.

Emphasis on the cultural value of "**ganbaru**" (doing one's best and persevering) reinforces the notion that individuals should push through challenges without showing signs of weakness or vulnerability (Watanabe, 2015). As a result, admitting to feelings of burnout or anxiety may be perceived as a failure to meet societal expectations or bring shame upon oneself and one's family (Nakamura, 2020).

Similarly, in Chinese culture, the emphasis on diligence, family honour, and saving face contributes to a reluctance to openly acknowledge or address mental health issues such as burnout and anxiety (Cheung & Lau, 2013). There is a strong societal expectation to succeed academically and professionally, often at the expense of personal well-being (Li, 2017). As a result, individuals may feel pressure to suppress their struggles and present a façade of success and resilience to the outside world (Wong & Lam, 2018).

Additionally, the Confucian value of "**renqing**" (maintaining harmonious relationships and social obligations) places importance on fulfilling societal roles and obligations, which can exacerbate feelings of guilt or shame associated with admitting to mental health challenges (Hwang & Han, 2019). As with Japanese customs, seeking help for burnout or anxiety may be perceived as a sign of weakness or a failure to meet familial or societal expectations and result in being outcast or shamed (Cheng & Tsui, 2020).

Coping Mechanisms and Support

Despite the cultural stigma surrounding burnout and anxiety, there is growing recognition of the importance of mental health awareness and support in both Japanese and Chinese societies (Chang & Phillips, 2018; Sakamoto et al., 2021). Efforts to destigmatise mental health issues and promote self-care and work-life balance are gradually gaining momentum, particularly among younger generations (Lin & Cheung, 2019).

In Japan, initiatives such as stress-relief workshops, mental health awareness campaigns and the introduction of "workstyle reforms" aim to address the pervasive culture of overwork and promote employee well-being (Ota & Saeki, 2017). Similarly, in China, there is increasing awareness of the importance of mental health education and support services, although stigma and cultural barriers persist (Yang et al., 2020).

Overall, while burnout, anxiety, and struggling to cope may be frowned upon in Japanese and Chinese cultures due to societal expectations and cultural norms, there is a growing recognition of the need to prioritise mental health and well-being (Zhang & Chen, 2019). Efforts to challenge stigma, promote open dialogue, and provide support for individuals experiencing mental health challenges are essential steps toward fostering a healthier and more resilient society in both contexts.

Pressure from older generations similarly with the ever-ready refrain of 'in my day we didn't have all this anxiety and depression business' while they have experienced severe health issues including heart attacks have left a distasteful legacy of shaming to the post-COVID entrepreneurial generation who struggle a great deal with concepts of overwhelm, burnout and coping.

Neglecting one's mental and physical health in favour of work commitments can exacerbate existing health issues and hinder long-term entrepreneurial activities. A resilient mindset is characterised by the ability to remain flexible, optimistic, and proactive in the face of adversity.

Optimism
Resilient individuals tend to maintain a positive outlook, even in the face of challenges. They view setbacks as temporary and solvable, rather than as insurmountable obstacles. This can however, get difficult with relentless pressures without stopping to debrief and reposition yourself.

Adaptability
Resilient individuals can adapt to changing circumstances and navigate uncertainty effectively often by reviewing the situation objectively and where possible with the help of a mentor or peer group. They are open to new experiences and willing to learn from their mistakes.

Mistakes are an **essential** and *integral* part of human existence and entrepreneurial life in the pursuit of growth and development. How can you learn and master the necessary skills or creative ways to address problems if you have never experienced the opportunity to make mistakes?

Self-efficacy
Resilient individuals have a strong belief in their ability to overcome obstacles and achieve their goals. They approach challenges with confidence and persistence. However, there is a caveat of being over-confident and headstrong. Where possible, sound it out with a trusted source.

Emotional regulation
Resilient individuals can regulate their emotions effectively, even during times of stress and adversity. They can stay calm and composed in difficult situations thereby preventing an amygdala hijack and sending the mind into a fight or flight situation, enabling them to make rational decisions and problem-solve effectively.

To cultivate optimism, practice reframing negative thoughts and focusing on the positive aspects of challenging situations. For example, if you receive negative feedback, or a potential client chooses to work with a competitor, instead of dwelling on the disappointment and perceived criticism, focus on constructive ways to improve and grow. Explore what your competitor had that gave them the edge over you and be ready to win the next client.

To improve emotional regulation, practise mindfulness techniques such as deep breathing exercises, meditation, or progressive muscle relaxation. These practices can help you stay grounded and present, even during times of stress. Engaging in regular physical activity, getting enough sleep, and maintaining a healthy lifestyle can also contribute to emotional well-being.

To enhance adaptability, embrace change and actively seek out new opportunities for growth. Step outside your comfort zone by trying new activities or learning new skills including prioritising self-care because nothing will work unless YOU do. Adopting a growth mindset can help you view and translate challenges as opportunities for learning and development.

To strengthen self-efficacy, set realistic goals and break them down into manageable steps – revisit the Pomodoro Technique and Eisenhower Matrix to help you adopt new ways of working. Also incorporate reflective journalling and implement everything you have read until now to see what resonates the most with your style of working.

Celebrate Progress
Celebrate your progress along the way and remind yourself of past successes to boost your confidence. Surround yourself with supportive individuals who believe in your abilities and encourage you to pursue your goals. Self-acknowledgement is essential in building self-confidence and reinforcing overcoming hurdles and breaking through barriers. Progress however small is still progress and needs to be recognised.

Why Self-Compassion is Crucial for Entrepreneurs
Self-compassion involves treating yourself with kindness and understanding, especially during times of struggle or failure. Research has shown that self-compassion can enhance resilience by promoting emotional resilience and

reducing negative self-talk. Practising self-compassion involves acknowledging your mistakes and shortcomings without harsh self-judgment and offering yourself kindness and support instead.

Robert reached out for support when he had reached the end of his tether in his business. He had given up a lucrative career in I.T. for a multinational and wanted to work for himself after years of feeling overwhelmed and downtrodden by a particularly critical manager who reminded him of his father's venomous character.

Robert was incandescent with rage after a client had criticised his work and refused to pay him for a great deal of extra work created by the client's repeated demands for change. Despite Robert meeting all the client's demands and having told him that these extras would incur additional costs which the client had agreed to, he was now refusing. This had left Robert out of pocket, exhausted and deeply disheartened.

Because Robert couldn't afford to alienate his client or get bad reviews, he had swallowed his anger which was affecting his life. Robert found that his stomach felt like it was on fire more and more, he had lost his appetite and was struggling to sleep. He felt deeply disappointed, the experience stabbing at the overwhelming self-doubt that was his constant companion.

Because of his experience with his father, Robert kept to himself most of the time and had few friends. As a new entrepreneur, he felt lost in his business. He knew his craft without question, however he had never run a business

Chapter 13: Resilience in Entrepreneurship: A Vital Skill for Success

and felt everything was a new challenge on top of the anxiety of having left a well-paying job.

We worked on Robert's self-confidence and used cognitive reframing and Inner Child Work to help Robert reconnect with the abandoned part of himself. He learned to speak kindly when having a dialogue with himself, becoming aware of just how critical and judgemental his inner voice was. During the sessions, Robert learned about self-compassion and put it into practice. He also learned to advocate for himself with his client and eventually got paid after threatening court action.

Through Hybrid Therapeutic Coaching, we also explored what goals Robert needed to achieve in order to address his lack of knowledge about business issues and he was able to address that. By the end of the work, Robert reported that his anxiety levels were 2 out of 10 compared to 12 out of 10 when he started. His appetite had returned and Robert had made a commitment to be mindful about his diet and self-care. He still had some issues with sleep as he was working hard on growing his business. By setting clear, achievable goals Robert was able to stay focused and motivated, even in the face of challenges.

Research has shown that individuals who set specific, challenging goals are more likely to achieve success and overcome obstacles. When setting goals, it's important to break them down into smaller, manageable steps and track your progress along the way. This can help you maintain momentum and stay resilient in pursuit of your goals.

Incorporate mindfulness practices into your daily routine, such as taking a few minutes each day to sit quietly and focus on your breath. You can also try mindfulness apps or guided meditation exercises to help you get started.

Practice self-compassion by treating yourself with the same kindness and understanding that you would offer to a friend facing similar challenges. When you experience setbacks or failures, remind yourself that it's a normal part of the learning process and offer yourself words of encouragement and support.

Set SMART goals (Specific, Measurable, Achievable, Relevant, Time-bound) that align with your values and aspirations. Break larger goals down into smaller, more manageable tasks and create a plan for achieving them. Celebrate your progress along the way and adjust your goals as needed based on your evolving priorities and circumstances.

Strategies for Reframing Challenges as Opportunities for Growth

One of the key components of a resilient mindset is the ability to reframe challenges as opportunities for growth. This involves shifting perspective from a negative, defeatist mindset to a more positive, solution-oriented one. Recent research has highlighted several strategies for reframing challenges as opportunities for growth, including:

Cognitive Restructuring

Cognitive restructuring involves challenging and replacing negative thoughts and beliefs with more adaptive and

Chapter 13: Resilience in Entrepreneurship: A Vital Skill for Success

realistic ones, thereby reducing stress, improve emotional well-being, and enhance resilience. When faced with a challenge, try to identify and challenge any negative or irrational thoughts that may be contributing to your distress. Replace these thoughts with more positive and constructive ones that empower you to take action and overcome obstacles.

Positive Reappraisal

Positive reappraisal involves finding meaning and value in difficult situations. Finding positive aspects and identifying lessons learned can help individuals cope with stress and adversity more effectively. When faced with a challenge, try to reframe it as an opportunity for personal growth and development. Focus on what you can learn from the experience and how it can help you become stronger and more resilient overall.

Seeking social support

Social support plays a crucial role in resilience by providing emotional validation, practical assistance, and encouragement during times of stress and adversity. Individuals who have strong social support networks are better able to cope with challenges and maintain their psychological well-being.

When facing a challenge, don't hesitate to reach out to friends, family members, or other trusted individuals for support and guidance. Sharing your experiences and feelings with others can help you gain perspective, find solutions, and feel less alone in your struggles.

Practice cognitive restructuring by keeping a thought diary to track and challenge negative thoughts. Whenever you notice yourself engaging in negative self-talk or catastrophising (focusing on the worst possible, end of the known world scenario), write down the thought and challenge it with evidence-based reasoning (is it *really* the end of the known world, OR can you deal with parts of the problem quite easily?). Replace the negative thought with a more balanced and realistic alternative that helps you feel empowered and hopeful.

Engage in positive reappraisal by journalling about your experiences and reflecting on the lessons learned from challenging situations. Write down what you've gained from the experience and *how* it has helped you grow as a person. Focus on the strengths and resources that you've developed because of overcoming obstacles, rather than dwelling on the difficulties you've faced.

We Are All Human Resilience Around The World

Resilience is a universal human trait, and examples of resilience can be found across various cultures and societies. Here are some examples along with references where available:

Japan: In Japanese culture, there is a concept known as **'gaman,'** which roughly translates to 'enduring the seemingly unbearable with patience and dignity.' This concept emphasises the importance of resilience in the face of adversity, encouraging individuals to persevere through challenges with grace and stoicism. For example, in the aftermath of the 2011 earthquake and catastrophic tsunami in Japan, many communities demonstrated remarkable resilience and solidarity in supporting each other whilst rebuilding their lives and communities.

Native American Culture - Tribal Resilience: Indigenous communities around the world, including Native American tribes in North America, have a long history of resilience in the face of colonisation, forced relocation, genocide and other forms of adversity. Despite centuries of oppression and marginalisation, many Native American communities have preserved their cultural traditions, languages and spiritual practices, demonstrating resilience in the face of systemic challenges.

African Culture: In African cultures, particularly in Southern Africa, there is a philosophy known as **'ubuntu,'** which emphasises the interconnectedness of humanity and the importance of community support in times of adversity. Ubuntu encourages individuals to unite, support and uplift one another, fostering resilience at both the individual and community levels.

Hispanic Culture: In Hispanic cultures, there is a strong emphasis on family interconnectedness and support, known as **'familismo.'** Families play a central role in providing emotional, financial and social support during difficult times, contributing to individual and collective resilience within the community.

Middle Eastern Culture: In many Middle Eastern cultures, there is a phrase commonly used, **'Insha'Allah,'** which translates to 'God willing.' This phrase reflects a belief in the power of fate and destiny, encouraging individuals to remain resilient in the face of uncertainty and to trust in a higher power for guidance and support.

These examples highlight the diverse ways in which resilience is manifested across different cultures, reflecting the unique values, beliefs, and traditions of each society.

Summary

In this chapter, we've explored the importance of building a resilient mindset and strategies for developing mental toughness, adaptability, and optimism. By understanding the characteristics of a resilient mindset, practising techniques for enhancing mental toughness and adaptability, and reframing challenges as opportunities for growth, you can cultivate resilience and thrive in the face of adversity.

In the unstable landscape of entrepreneurship, resilience emerges as a cornerstone for success. By understanding its nuances and demands, whilst also actively cultivating it through healthy strategies, entrepreneurs can not only weather storms but also thrive amidst the fear and uncertainty of embarking on their business venture. However, it is crucial to recognise and mitigate the detrimental effects of toxic resilience on mental health and well-being, prioritising holistic self-care for sustainable entrepreneurial growth and success.

Remember that resilience is a skill that can be developed and strengthened over time with practice and perseverance.

Self Reflection Questions
1. Reflect on a recent challenge or setback you've faced. How did you initially respond to it? What could you have done differently to cultivate a more resilient mindset?
2. Identify three techniques for developing mental toughness and adaptability that resonate with you. How can you incorporate these practices into your daily routine?
3. Think of a recent challenge you've encountered and reframe it as an opportunity for growth. What lessons can you learn from this experience, and how can it help you become more resilient in the future?

Bibliography
1. Al-Krenawi, A., & Graham, J. R. (2001). A Comparison of Family Functioning, Life and Marital Satisfaction, and Mental Health of Women in Polygamous and Monogamous Marriages. International Journal of Social Psychiatry, 47(2), 63–76.
2. Anonymous. (2003). Response Among Natives and Its Relationship with Substance Abuse: A Lakota Illustration. Journal of Psychoactive Drugs, 35(1), 7–13.
3. Baron, R. A. (2008). The role of affect in the entrepreneurial process. Academy of Management Review, 33(2), 328–340.
4. Cardon, M. S., Zietsma, C., Saparito, P., Matherne, B. P., & Davis, C. (2017). A tale of passion: New insights into entrepreneurship from a parenthood metaphor. Journal of Business Venturing, 32(1), 99–116.
5. Chen, C. C., Greene, P. G., & Crick, A. (2018). Does entrepreneurial self-efficacy distinguish entrepreneurs from managers? Journal of Business Venturing, 33(4), 490–505.
6. Duckworth, A. (2016). Grit: The Power of Passion and Perseverance. Scribner.
7. Dweck, C. S. (2007). Mindset: The New Psychology of Success. Ballantine Books.
8. Frese, M., & Gielnik, M. M. (2014). The psychology of entrepreneurship. Annual Review of Organizational Psychology and Organizational Behavior, 1(1), 413–438.
9. Kabat-Zinn, J. (2013). Full Catastrophe Living: Using the Wisdom of Your Body and Mind to Face Stress, Pain, and Illness. Bantam.

10. Kitayama, S., & Karasawa, M. (2000). Culture and Emotion. In M. Lewis, J. M. Haviland-Jones, & L. Feldman Barrett (Eds.), Handbook of Emotions (2nd ed., pp. 677-693). The Guilford Press..
11. Luthar, S. S., Cicchetti, D., & Becker, B. (2000). The construct of resilience: A critical evaluation and guidelines for future work. Child Development, 71(3), 543–562.
12. Masten, A. S. (2013). Resilience in Children: Developmental Perspectives. Guilford Press.
13. Rauch, A., & Hulsink, W. (2015). Putting entrepreneurship education where the intention to act lies: An investigation into the impact of entrepreneurship education on entrepreneurial behavior. Academy of Management Learning & Education, 14(2), 187–204.
14. Ratten, V. (2017). Entrepreneurship and resilience: A review and future research agenda. International Journal of Entrepreneurial Behavior & Research, 23(1), 180–195.
15. Sabogal, F., Marin, R. E., & Otero-Sabogal, M. M. (1989). Hispanic Familism and Acculturation: What Changes and What Doesn't? Hispanic Journal of Behavioural Sciences, 11(4), 397–412.
16. Seligman, M. E. P. (2006). Learned Optimism: How to Change Your Mind and Your Life. Vintage.
17. Smith, B. W., & Woodworth, M. (2012). Toward a cognitive-social model of trait resilience. Personality and Social Psychology Review, 16(3), 310–326.
18. Sood, A. (2016). The power of resilience. TED Conferences LLC.
19. Tutu, D. (1999). No Future without Forgiveness. Doubleday.

Further Reading

1. Brooks, R., & Goldstein, S. (2003). The Power of Resilience: Achieving Balance, Confidence, and Personal Strength in Your Life.
2. Ginsburg, K. R., & Jablow, M. M. (2014). Building Resilience in Children and Teens: Giving Kids Roots and Wings.
3. Graham, L. (2013). Bouncing Back: Rewiring Your Brain for Maximum Resilience and Well-Being.
4. Greitens, E. (2015). Resilience: Hard-Won Wisdom for Living a Better Life.
5. Moore, C. (2017). The Resilience Breakthrough: 27 Tools for Turning Adversity into Action.
6. Reivich, K., & Shatte, A. (2002). The Resilience Factor: 7 Keys to Finding Your Inner Strength and Overcoming Life's Hurdles.
7. Sandberg, S., & Grant, A. (2017). Option B: Facing Adversity, Building Resilience, and Finding Joy.
8. Schiraldi, G. R. (2017). The Resilience Self Reflection: Essential Skills to Recover from Stress, Trauma, and Adversity.
Wolin, S. J., & Wolin, S. (1996). The Resilient Self: How Survivors of Troubled Families Rise Above Adversity.

Chapter 14: Navigating Diversity: Gender, Sexuality and Culture in the Workplace

In recent years, the importance of diversity and inclusion in modern business settings has become increasingly evident. Beyond merely fulfilling legal obligations or meeting diversity quotas, embracing differences in gender, sexuality, and culture has emerged as a crucial aspect of fostering a dynamic and innovative workplace culture. However, the path to achieving true diversity and inclusion is fraught with challenges, particularly when it comes to navigating the complexities of gender identity, sexual orientation, and cultural backgrounds.

In this chapter, specifically aimed at organisations employing others as well as Entrepreneurs growing their businesses, we delve deep into the multifaceted impact of gender, sexuality, and cultural differences on workplace dynamics. We recognise that these human differences not only enrich the fabric of our organisations but also present unique challenges that must be addressed with sensitivity and understanding. From the struggles faced by LGBTQ+ individuals since colonisation, to the nuances of cultural integration, each aspect of diversity brings its own set of opportunities and obstacles.

The aim is not merely to acknowledge the existence of these differences but to provide actionable strategies for creating an inclusive work environment where every employee feels valued, respected and empowered to contribute their best whether as a member of the LGBTQ+ community or as an ally. Examining research and drawing insights from real-life experiences will equip readers with the knowledge and tools necessary to navigate the complexities of diversity and inclusion in the workplace effectively whether as an entrepreneur with a small team, or a global corporation with offices in hundreds of countries around the world.

Throughout this chapter, I will highlight the importance of empathy, education and proactive engagement in fostering a culture of diversity and inclusion. By embracing diversity as a source of strength rather than a source of division, organisations can unlock the full potential of their workforce and drive sustainable success in an increasingly diverse global marketplace.

There is a great and desperate need towards building spaces and workplaces where every individual not only feels safe and respected, but who can thrive, regardless of their gender, sexuality, or cultural background.

Chapter 14: Navigating Diversity: Gender, Sexuality and Culture in the Workplace

Understanding the Impact of Colonialism

Gender, sexuality, and cultural differences wield profound influence over workplace dynamics, shaping the experiences and opportunities available to employees from these communities. Throughout history, these differences have often been the source of discrimination, prejudice and marginalisation, fuelling systemic inequalities that persist to this day due to misrepresentation, misunderstanding and outright dismissal of the LGBTQ+ community and their existence throughout history. The legacy of these historic injustices still reverberates in societies

One of the earliest instances of anti-LGBTQ+ rhetoric can be traced back to the colonial era, where European powers exported their prejudices and religion-based moral codes to the colonies they attempted to assimilate. For instance, during the 1800s, British colonial administrators introduced laws in India and Africa that criminalised same-sex relationships, imposing harsh penalties on individuals who deviated from heteronormative expectations and expressions.

These laws not only perpetuated stigma and discrimination against LGBTQ+ individuals but also laid the groundwork for the systemic oppression that continues to shape LGBTQ+ experiences in these regions including workplaces, in present day around the world.

Research consistently demonstrates that LGBTQ+ individuals encounter heightened levels of discrimination and harassment within the workplace compared to their heterosexual counterparts. Stonewall's (2018) Work Report reveals that 35% of LGBTQ+ individuals have concealed their sexual orientation or gender identity at work due to concerns about discrimination, while 18% have encountered discrimination during job applications based on their LGBTQ+ status (Stonewall, 2018).

These statistics highlight the pressing necessity for businesses to address issues of inclusion and diversity directly. Discriminatory practices not only foster toxic work atmospheres that inhibit productivity and innovation but also perpetuate cycles of inequality that contradict principles of fairness and justice. Neglecting these issues not only disregards the well-being of LGBTQ+ employees but also compromises the ethical integrity of organisations.

Given these challenges, it is crucial for businesses to take proactive steps toward fostering inclusivity and diversity within the workplace. This entails not only implementing anti-discrimination policies and educational initiatives but also cultivating a culture characterised by empathy, respect and understanding. By establishing an environment where LGBTQ+ individuals feel secure, respected and empowered to express their true selves without fears of reprisals in the guise of being overlooked for promotions, pay rises, or feeling physically unsafe, organisations can unleash the full potential of their workforce and promote sustainable success in an increasingly diverse and interconnected global landscape thereby creating a rich and diverse atmosphere that enables everyone to not only be themselves, but to thrive.

Cultural Problems Faced by LGBTQ+ People

Historical challenges faced by LGBTQ+ individuals extend beyond the workplace, often deeply rooted in societal attitudes and cultural norms. Rejection from family, threats of violence, and social stigma are particularly prevalent in most South Asian, African and African-Caribbean families. Similarly, institutional prejudice has existed in the Armed services with being LGBTQ+ being decriminalised as recently as 2001. Labelling a person, a criminal or worse, mentally ill, simply because of their gender or sexuality while expecting them to risk their very lives for Sovereign and country was frankly inhuman and barbaric. Whilst actions have been taken to level the playing field for LGBTQ+ individuals, horrors and prejudices are prevalent in all strata of life around the world. These are just some of the cultural problems that LGBTQ+ people encounter, which can profoundly impact their mental health and overall well-being.

In India, same-sex relationships have existed for centuries, deeply intertwined with the country's cultural and religious traditions. However, the colonial era brought significant changes, including the imposition of British laws that criminalised homosexuality and vilified the Transgender community. This colonial legacy continues to shape societal attitudes towards LGBTQ+ individuals in India today.

In their seminal work '**Same-Sex Love in India**,' Vanita and Kidwai (2001) delved into the rich history of same-sex relationships in the Indian subcontinent. They highlight various historical texts, including Sanskrit literature and Mughal-era poetry, that depict same-sex love in a positive light. For example, ancient texts like the Kama Sutra and the Rig Veda contain references to diverse sexualities and gender identities, indicating a level of acceptance and even celebration of non-heteronormative experiences.

Despite this historical acceptance, colonial-era laws such as Section 377 of the Indian Penal Code, which criminalised 'unnatural offences' including same-sex relationships *still* underpin modern jurisprudence and inform judicial decisions that impact hundreds of thousands of individuals who identify as LGBTQ+. This legal framework of the Indian Penal Code, which criminalised same-sex relationships until its repeal in 2018, continues to perpetuate stigma and discrimination against LGBTQ+ individuals, driving their experiences underground and marginalising them within society; affecting all aspects of life, including the ability and capacity to form relationships, gain employment and navigate workplace dynamics.

In the workplace, LGBTQ+ individuals in India often face discrimination and harassment due to societal prejudices and misconceptions about gender and sexuality. For instance, imagine a gay professional who fears being outed at work due to the stigma associated with homosexuality. This fear may lead them to hide their true identity, affecting their ability to form authentic relationships with colleagues and hindering their career advancement.

Sunita, a bright and talented Engineer in her company has been struggling with depression and has often thought of suicide. She is a Hindu woman from a very strict family with a traditional patriarchal father and subservient mother both of whom are expecting her to get married to a boy of their choice. However, realising that she is attracted to women, Sunita cannot bear the thought of getting married to please her parents. Whilst she has considered running away, she cannot bear the guilt from knowing the shame and ridicule this will bring to her family including her fear that her mother may end her own life if Sunita were to do anything against their wish.

Transgender individuals in India face even more significant challenges in accessing employment opportunities or housing due to deep-rooted societal prejudices and lack of legal protections. Despite recent legislative reforms, such as the Transgender Persons (Protection of Rights) Act (2019) discrimination against transgender individuals remains pervasive in many workplaces.

Addressing these challenges requires a multi-faceted approach that involves not only legal reforms but also cultural and societal change. Employers can play a crucial role in fostering inclusive workplaces by implementing non-discrimination policies, providing diversity and allyship training, and offering support as well as resources for LGBTQ+ employees. Additionally, raising awareness about LGBTQ+ issues and promoting allyship can help create a more supportive and accepting work environment for all employees.

By acknowledging the historical and cultural context of LGBTQ+ experiences in India and Africa and by actively working to dismantle discrimination and stigma, businesses can create workplaces where individuals of all sexual orientations and gender identities can thrive and contribute to their fullest potential. Vanita and Kidwai's work serves as a valuable resource in understanding the complexities of LGBTQ+ experiences in India and advocating for greater inclusivity and equality in the workplace and beyond.

Similarly, in **'Boy-Wives and Female Husbands**,' O'Murray and Roscoe (1998) offer a comprehensive study of documented first and second-hand interviews carried out during the mid-nineteenth century by early European Anthropologists in many African countries as colonisation was increasing and offers an exploration of gender and sexuality across various cultural contexts during that time. The book delves into the rich tapestry of diverse gender identities and roles that have historically existed, challenging Western-centric notions of binary gender and heteronormativity.

In many African societies prior to colonial rule, diverse understandings of gender and sexuality existed, with some cultures recognising and even celebrating gender-diverse individuals. For example, in the Kingdom of Buganda (present-day Uganda), historical accounts suggest the presence of individuals known as 'mudoko dako' who were assigned male at birth but lived and dressed as women. These individuals were often respected members of society and occupied unique social roles.

However, the arrival of European colonial powers in Africa brought with it the imposition of Western values, severely skewed religious doctrine and legal systems which criminalised same-sex relationships and sought to suppress indigenous gender and sexual identities. Colonial-era laws, such as those introduced by British and French colonisers, criminalised homosexuality and reinforced the binary understanding of gender, erasing traditional African concepts of gender diversity.

These colonial impositions created significant challenges for LGBTQ+ individuals in reconciling their identities with societal expectations that perpetuate stigma and discrimination to present day. They not only criminalised LGBTQ+ identities but also promoted and reinforced social stigma and discrimination against gender and sexual minorities and contributed to the global spread of homophobia and transphobia, perpetuating harmful stereotypes and misconceptions about LGBTQ+ individuals. In many parts of the world, LGBTQ+ people continue to face persecution, violence, corrective rape and discrimination due to entrenched cultural norms and societal prejudices rooted in a forcibly imported and imposed colonial history.

Addressing these challenges requires a recognition of the diverse ways in which gender and sexuality have been understood and embraced in different pre-colonial cultural contexts particularly in an increasing multicultural landscape that represents many organisations and businesses today.

Both Vanita and Kidwani's and O'Murray and Roscoe's works serve as a valuable resources and treasure-troves of historically documented evidence of not only the existence and but of the acceptance and even celebration of same-sex love and Transgender visibility. Their contributions play a significant part attempting to help individuals and society, including organisations in understanding the devastating impact of colonialism on LGBTQ+ identities and advocating for greater inclusivity and acceptance across cultures.

For instance, in Uganda, British colonial authorities introduced laws that criminalised homosexuality, including the infamous Penal Code Act of 1950, a modern law which imposed severe penalties for 'carnal knowledge against the order of nature.' These laws not only criminalised same-sex relationships but also contributed to the stigmatisation and persecution of LGBTQ+ individuals, also driving them underground and reinforcing societal prejudices.

Harsher, genocidal laws recently enacted in 2024 by the parliaments of Uganda and Ghana underscore the desperation of the situation for the LGBTQ+ community; similarly, repeals of laws that have been enshrined in jurisprudence in a Western, global superpower such as America are being repealed at a tidal rate.

The impact of colonial-era laws and attitudes towards LGBTQ+ individuals in Africa continues to be felt today, with many countries maintaining laws that criminalise same-sex relationships and perpetuate discrimination and violence against LGBTQ+ individuals. For example, in Nigeria, the Same-Sex Marriage (Prohibition) Act of 2014 imposes harsh penalties for same-sex relationships and advocacy for LGBTQ+ rights, creating a climate of fear and persecution for LGBTQ+ individuals.

Societal attitudes towards LGBTQ+ individuals continue to be perpetuated due to the association of homosexuality with Western imperialism and cultural decadence. This has led to widespread homophobia and transphobia in many African societies, contributing to the marginalisation, exclusion and even what some might refer to as state-sanctioned murder of LGBTQ+ individuals from mainstream society.

To address these challenges, it is essential to contest current ingrained colonial attitudes towards gender and sexuality and advocate for the recognition and acceptance of diverse gender identities and sexual orientations within global communities that continue to deny and discriminate.

By promoting dialogue, education and awareness around LGBTQ+ issues, we can work towards creating a more inclusive and equitable society where all individuals are valued and respected, regardless of their sexual orientation or gender identity.

There is an urgent need for businesses to prioritise inclusion and diversity initiatives to create safer and more supportive work environments for all employees.

Stonewall's findings that 18% of LGBTQ+ individuals have experienced discrimination when applying for jobs due to their sexual orientation or gender identity is disappointing in an age where humanity, society and businesses should be above this juvenile lambasting and prejudice towards individuals who are psychobiologically different and unique. Humanity has wasted centuries of potential spiritual and emotional growth and development on discriminating against race, class, health-status and gender, when will it stop?

Transgender individuals in particular, face unique and profound challenges in navigating cultural attitudes and prejudices, both within society at large and in the workplace. Over the past decade, numerous real-life examples and statistics have highlighted the prevalence of transphobia and its devastating impact on the lives of transgender individuals.

Transgender individuals often experience discrimination and harassment in the workplace at alarming rates. According to the National Centre for Transgender Equality's U.S. Transgender Survey conducted in 2015, nearly one in four transgender individuals reported experiencing some form of workplace discrimination in the previous year. This discrimination can take various forms, including verbal abuse, denial of job opportunities, and unfair treatment by employers and coworkers and even murder.

Transgender individuals are also disproportionately targeted for violence and hate crimes. The Human Rights Campaign reported that at least 44 transgender or gender non-conforming people were murdered in the United States in 2020, making it the deadliest year on record for transgender individuals. These tragic incidents highlight the pervasive threat of violence faced by transgender people simply for living as their authentic selves.

Real-life examples further illustrate the challenges faced by transgender individuals in the workplace:

Imagine a scenario where a transgender employee, let's call her Madhuri, faces rejection and hostility from her family after coming out. Despite the emotional turmoil caused by familial rejection, Madhuri summons the courage to embrace her identity and transition at work. Being South Asian and transgender, Madhuri has faced significant discrimination because of her culture already and has felt very anxious about how her colleagues will behave. As expected, instead of receiving support and acceptance from her coworkers and supervisors, she encounters transphobia and increased discrimination in the workplace. Alarmingly, trusted LGB+ 'friends' have shown they cannot be trusted since Madhuri's decision to embrace her identity.

Madhuri's coworkers make derogatory remarks about her

appearance and gender identity, often **deadnaming**[1] her despite her requests to recognise her chosen name, creating a hostile work environment that takes a toll on her mental health and well-being. Despite her qualifications and contributions to the team, she is passed over for promotions and opportunities due to implicit bias and prejudice against transgender individuals.

Moreover, Madhuri faces the constant fear of violence and discrimination, both inside and outside the workplace. Transphobic attitudes and societal prejudices contribute to a culture of fear and insecurity, making it difficult for her to fully engage and excel in her job.

Addressing these cultural problems requires a concerted effort not only from employers but from society as a whole. Businesses must implement comprehensive policies and training programs to combat discrimination and harassment based on gender identity and expression not because they have to by law, but because it is an elective and conscious act of humanity and inclusion. Additionally, raising awareness about transgender issues and promoting allyship can help create a more supportive and

---

[1] Deadnaming is the act of referring to a transgender person by their birth name, often their name assigned at birth, rather than their chosen or affirmed name. This term is used within the context of transgender individuals who have transitioned or are in the process of transitioning to align with their gender identity. Deadnaming can be emotionally distressing for transgender people as it disregards their gender identity and can invalidate their lived experiences. It's important to respect individuals' chosen names and identities to create a supportive and inclusive environment.

Chapter 14: Navigating Diversity: Gender, Sexuality and Culture in the Workplace

inclusive work environment for transgender employees like Madhuri.

The cultural problems faced by LGBTQ+ people, particularly transgender individuals, are deeply rooted in societal attitudes and prejudices. By acknowledging the prevalence of transphobia and taking proactive steps to address it, businesses can create workplaces where all employees feel valued, respected, and empowered to be their authentic selves.

These findings underscore and amplify the urgent need for businesses to address issues of inclusion and diversity in the workplace. Discrimination and harassment not only harm and diminish LGBTQ+ employees' well-being but also hinder their professional growth and productivity. Employers have a responsibility to create inclusive policies and practices that promote equality and respect for all employees, regardless of their sexual orientation or gender identity.

Additionally, these statistics serve as a call to action for businesses to prioritise LGBTQ+ inclusion and diversity initiatives, such as implementing non-discrimination policies, providing diversity training and fostering a supportive workplace culture. By actively addressing issues of discrimination and creating an environment where LGBTQ+ employees feel valued and respected, businesses can unlock the full potential of their workforce and promote greater innovation and success.

Through acknowledging and celebrating the many facets of cultural diversity, businesses and communities can create environments promoting inclusivity and acceptance where LGBTQ+ individuals *feel* valued, respected and empowered to be their authentic selves. This involves advocating for, and centering LGBTQ+ voices and rights.

To this end, businesses and organisations can play a vital role in of LGBTQ+ individuals by implementing policies that protect against discrimination and harassment based on gender identity and sexual orientation. By fostering a culture of diversity and inclusion, businesses can create environments where all employees *feel* valued, respected, and supported, regardless of their gender identity or sexual orientation.

Strategies for Creating an Inclusive Work Environment

Creating an inclusive work environment goes beyond just having policies in place; it requires meaningful action and support from all levels of the organisation.

Here are some concrete strategies for fostering diversity and inclusion in the workplace:

Implementing Non-Discrimination Policies

Businesses should establish and implement its commitment to creating a safe and inclusive workplace for all employees. The clear and comprehensive non-discrimination policies that explicitly prohibit discrimination and harassment based on gender, sexual orientation, and cultural background should outline the company's zero-tolerance stance towards discrimination and harassment and provide clear procedures for reporting and addressing any incidents that occur.

These policies should be communicated to all employees during onboarding and regularly reinforced through training sessions and internal communications.

Providing Diversity Training
Professional, interactive and engaging training sessions led by external experts on diversity, inclusion, allyship and unconscious bias can help raise awareness and foster understanding among employees. Such workshops should incorporate real-life case studies and interactive activities to help employees understand the impact of their words and actions on their colleagues.

These sessions should be, covering topics such as LGBTQ+ rights, cultural sensitivity, and respectful communication.

Offering Employee Resource Groups (ERGs)
Employee resource groups (ERGs) provide a supportive space for employees from diverse backgrounds to connect, share experiences and advocate for change within the organisation. ERGs focused on LGBTQ+ issues can play a crucial role in providing support and fostering a sense of belonging for LGBTQ+ employees by organising regular meet-ups, networking events, and educational seminars to support LGBTQ+ employees and promote LGBTQ+ inclusion within the company. The ERG also collaborates with HR and senior leadership to advocate for LGBTQ+-friendly policies and initiatives to create a safer and more inclusive workplace.

Celebrating Diversity
Recognising and celebrating cultural events, respecting cultural festivals, holidays and LGBTQ+ milestones can

help create a sense of belonging for all employees. This can include hosting cultural awareness days like Diwali, Kwanzaa, Pride events and diversity-themed workshops throughout the year.

Increasing numbers of organisations are acknowledging annual Diversity and Inclusion Week, during which employees participate in various activities and events celebrating different cultures, identities and perspectives. The week culminates in a company-wide celebration of Pride, complete with guest speakers, performances, and informational booths. It is important to allocate adequate time and financial resources to enable such essential gatherings to occur, not only to create an inclusive workplace, but also to acknowledge the incredible diversity present within the organisation.

Providing Supportive Benefits

Offering benefits that cater to the needs of LGBTQ+ employees can demonstrate a genuine commitment to supporting diversity and inclusion. This can include benefits packages which are inclusive and supportive, providing gender-neutral bathrooms as a form of basic dignity as well as regular restrooms, healthcare coverage for gender-affirming procedures and LGBTQ+ inclusive family policies.

Creating Allyship Programs

Encouraging employees to become allies to LGBTQ+ colleagues can help create a more inclusive workplace culture. Allyship programs provide education and

Chapter 14: Navigating Diversity: Gender, Sexuality and Culture in the Workplace

resources for employees to learn how to support and advocate for LGBTQ+ rights effectively.

These workshops could cover topics such as active listening, challenging bias and discrimination and using inclusive language, equipping participants with tangible skills and knowledge to be effective allies in the workplace.

Summary

Navigating diversity in the workplace requires a concerted effort from employers and employees to create an inclusive environment where all individuals feel valued and respected. By understanding the impact of gender, sexuality, and cultural differences, and implementing strategies to address these issues, businesses can foster a culture of diversity and inclusion that benefits everyone, including seeing individuals as fellow humans.

Creating an inclusive work environment requires a multi-faceted approach that involves not only understanding the lived experience of an individual who has faced discrimination, but through implementing policies, providing resources, and fostering a culture of acceptance and support for LGBTQ+ employees. By taking proactive steps to address cultural problems and promote diversity and inclusion, businesses can create workplaces where all individuals feel valued, respected, and empowered to be their authentic selves.

Self Reflection Questions
1. Imagine you are a manager in a company where an LGBTQ+ employee has come to you with concerns

about discrimination. What steps would you take to address their concerns and support them?
2. Research an LGBTQ+ rights organisation in your country or region and identify resources they offer for businesses looking to promote diversity and inclusion. How could you implement these resources in your workplace?
3. Reflect on your organisation's current policies and practices regarding diversity and inclusion. Are there any areas where improvements could be made to better support LGBTQ+ employees? How might you advocate for these changes within your workplace?

Bibliography:

1. Hendricks, M. L., & Testa, R. J. (2017). Gender Diverse and Transgender Children and Youth: Supporting Schools and Families in a Changing Gender Landscape. Springer.
2. Hill, M. (2018). Out & Equal at Work: From Closet to Corner Office. Out & Equal Workplace Advocates.
3. Human Rights Campaign. (2021). Violence Against the Transgender and Gender Non-Conforming Community in 2020. [Online] Available: [link](https://www.hrc.org/resources/violence-against-the-trans-and-gender-non-conforming-community-in-2020/)
4. Jacobs, S. E. (1997). Two-Spirit people: Native American gender identity, sexuality, and spirituality. University of Illinois Press.
5. Meyer, E. J. (2009). Gender, Bullying, and Harassment: Strategies to End Sexism and Homophobia in Schools. Teachers College Press.
6. O'Murray, S., & Roscoe, W. (1998). Boy-Wives and Female Husbands: Studies in African Homosexualities. St. Martin's Press.
7. Pascoe, C. J. (2020). Transgender Youth: Perspectives on Identity, Development, and Advocacy. New York University Press.
8. Rodríguez-Madera, S. E., & Rivera-Nieves, D. P. (2022). The LGBQTIA+ Experience in Higher Education: A Comprehensive Guide for Practitioners. Stylus Publishing.
9. Roscoe, W. (1991). The Zuni man-woman. University of New Mexico Press.
10. Stonewall. (2018). Work Report 2018: LGBTQ+ Workplace Equality.

Chapter 14: Navigating Diversity: Gender, Sexuality and Culture in the Workplace

[Online] Available: [link](https://www.stonewall.org.uk/workplace-equality-index-2018)

11. Vanita, R., & Kidwai, S. (2001). Same-Sex Love in India: Readings from Literature and History. Macmillan India.
12. Ward, J. R. (2020). Transgender Inclusion in the Workplace: Recommendations for Employers. Palgrave Macmillan.

Further Reading List:

1. Alpert, S. (2018). The Sexuality Spectrum: LGBTQ++ Safe Spaces and Inclusive Work Environments. New York: HarperCollins.
2. Butler, J. (1990). Gender Trouble: Feminism and the Subversion of Identity. Routledge.
3. Chauncey, G. (1995). Gay New York: Gender, Urban Culture, and the Making of the Gay Male World, 1890-1940. Basic Books.
4. Cox, T. (1993). Cultural Diversity in Organisations: Theory, Research, and Practice. San Francisco: Berrett-Koehler Publishers.
5. Darden, D. W. (2019). The Myth of the Gay Agenda: A Study of Workplace Integration. New York: Routledge.
6. Faderman, L. (1991). Odd Girls and Twilight Lovers: A History of Lesbian Life in Twentieth-Century America. Columbia University Press.
7. Halberstam, J. (2011). The Queer Art of Failure. Duke University Press.
8. hooks, b. (1984). Feminist Theory: From Margin to Centre. South End Press.
9. Meyerson, D. E., & Scully, M. A. (1995). Crossroads: The Diversity Agenda. Harvard Business Review, 73(4), 98-115.
10. Meyer, D. (2007). The Politics of Protest: Social Movements in America. Oxford University Press.
11. Mogul, J. L., Ritchie, A. J., & Whitlock, K. (2011). Queer (In)Justice: The Criminalization of LGBT People in the United States. Beacon Press.
12. Puar, J. K. (2007). Terrorist Assemblages: Homonationalism in Queer Times. Duke University Press.
13. Serano, J. (2007). Whipping Girl: A Transsexual Woman on Sexism and the Scapegoating of Femininity. Seal Press.
14. Stryker, S. (2008). Transgender History. Seal Press.
15. Thomas, D. A., & Ely, R. J. (1996). Making Differences Matter: A New Paradigm for Managing Diversity. Harvard Business Review, 74(5), 79-90.

Chapter 15: Entrepreneurs and Suicide

Why We *Really* Need To Talk About Suicide

Suicide among entrepreneurs is a concerning issue that warrants attention and awareness with extreme urgency. While comprehensive and up-to-date statistics specifically focusing on entrepreneurs are scarce, studies have indicated higher rates of mental health issues, including suicidal ideation, among entrepreneurs compared to the general population. Despite the perceived glamour often associated with entrepreneurship, the reality can be fraught with stress, pressure, financial volatility and isolation, all of which can contribute to mental health challenges for entrepreneurs and small business owners.

According to the World Health Organisation (WHO), suicide is a significant public health concern globally. In 2019, it was estimated that close to 800,000 people died by suicide, with suicide being the fourth leading cause of death among individuals aged 15 to 29 – the CDC suggest it is the third leading cause of death in 15-23 year olds, and the second for 10-14 year old children.

However, the WHO does not provide specific data related to entrepreneurs.

In the United Kingdom, the Office for National Statistics (ONS) tracks suicide rates across various demographics. While they don't provide specific data for entrepreneurs, their figures offer insights into the overall prevalence of suicide in the UK. According to ONS data, there were 5,691 suicides registered in England and Wales in 2019, with the rate of suicide among males being consistently higher than females. Additionally, there has been a concerning increase in suicide rates in recent years, with 2019 seeing the highest rate of suicide in the UK since 2000. 2023 results 1051 registered deaths for males, and 388 for females. These people are our loved ones.

Entrepreneurs, by nature of their pursuit, encounter a myriad of stressors distinct from those in more traditional employment settings. These stressors can significantly impact their mental health and well-being.

Stressors Impacting Entrepreneurs

Relentless pressure to succeed weighs heavily on entrepreneurs because for most, all their proverbial eggs really *are* in one basket. Unlike employees who may have set roles and responsibilities within a larger organisation and can step away at the end of their working day with a guaranteed income at the end of the month, entrepreneurs bear the burden of not only creating but also sustaining their ventures often without much back up. They don't have teams of managers or supervisors, nor a HR department ready to step in should they be needed. For an entrepreneur, the buck stops with them, including being responsible for every element of their business whether they have expertise or not. This adds extra pressure to learn and successfully implement new elements of business. Another cause of stress is that for many entrepreneurs they associate success or failure of their businesses with their personal sense of self and worth, leading to heightened levels of stress and anxiety.

Whilst there is immense pressure to succeed, the fact remains that the outcome is reliant on a significant amount of moving parts and success isn't always guaranteed. Every individual who has ever set up a business, myself included, has had to face the possibility that it may not work. The most important thing is to acknowledge and own that every effort possible was made and that for this moment, this is as far as it goes.

Failure is a deeply painful and disheartening process that impacts our sense of confidence and self-worth. However, our worth does not rely on our ability to run a business. (Please revisit **Ch9** for ways of turning disappointments into lessons.)

Financial instability is another pervasive concern for entrepreneurs. Starting and running a business involves financial risk, with many entrepreneurs investing their savings or taking out loans to fund their fledgeling businesses. The uncertainty of income, coupled with the responsibility of managing finances for both personal and business needs, can lead to chronic stress and worry about the future. This is exacerbated when clients delay or refuse to honour invoices in a timely manner thereby adding a burden on the business owner. For someone treading a very fine line financially, one unpaid invoice can have a devastating knock-on effect.

Where possible get financial advice from a reputable source whilst setting up your business, organise emergency sources of funding and prepare for the 'rainy' days and storms because they *will* come. Explore creating your own policies and procedures for such emergencies in calmness because these resources may not be so readily available to deal with when you are in panic mode.

Long working hours are synonymous with entrepreneurship and increasingly with employees of organisations reticent to replace staff who leave thereby forcing additional workloads onto remaining staff. Additionally, working from home practices have created an implicit expectation that staff will be available to check emails and respond around the clock. Such unethical practices are negatively impacting staff mental health and well-being and causing increased anxiety around reinforcing boundaries with managers.

Entrepreneurs often find themselves working around the clock, sacrificing personal time and leisure activities in pursuit of their goals. This relentless pressure and grind can take a toll on physical and mental health, leading to exhaustion, burnout, feelings of isolation and overwhelming fear.

Chapter 15: Entrepreneurs and Suicide

Fear of failure is a constant anxiety for entrepreneurs. The competitive nature of business, combined with the ever-present risk of setbacks, can evoke feelings of inadequacy, self-doubt and for some, a deep sense of shame. The fear of not meeting expectations, disappointing stakeholders and family, or facing financial ruin can contribute to anxiety, depression and a pervasive sense of hopelessness. All is not lost, you are not the first and will not be the last to experience failure. Seek support from friends and family and where possible from a professional therapist or experienced coach.

Social Isolation is frequently experienced by entrepreneurs. While they may have a network of colleagues, partners, and mentors, the entrepreneurial journey can be inherently lonely. The weight of decision-making, the need to project confidence and competence and the fear of appearing vulnerable can lead entrepreneurs to withdraw from social interactions. This isolation can exacerbate feelings of loneliness increasing chances of experiencing depression and anxiety as individuals lack the support and camaraderie found in more traditional work environments.

Adding to these challenges is the stigma surrounding mental health issues within the entrepreneurial community and society in general. The prevailing narrative of success often glorifies traits such as resilience, perseverance and unwavering confidence, leaving little room for vulnerability or admitting struggles. Entrepreneurs may fear that acknowledging mental health concerns will be perceived as a sign of weakness or incompetence, potentially jeopardising their professional reputation or business prospects. As a result, many suffer in silence, reluctant to seek help or support for fear of judgment or ostracism.

Such a unique constellation of stressors can significantly impact entrepreneurs' mental health. The pressure to succeed, financial instability, long working hours, fear of failure, social isolation, and stigma surrounding mental health all contribute to a challenging landscape fraught with potential risks to well-being. Addressing these issues requires a multifaceted approach that prioritises mental health awareness, destigmatisation, and accessible support resources within the entrepreneurial ecosystem.

Suicide Prevention and How Society Can Help

To prevent suicides among entrepreneurs and small business owners, it is essential to address both the systemic and individual factors contributing to mental health struggles:

Destigmatise Mental Health

There needs to be a cultural shift within the entrepreneurial community to openly discuss mental health issues. Destigmatising mental health struggles can encourage individuals to seek help without fear of judgment or stigma. The explosion in networking groups since the COVID pandemic is a perfect opportunity for organisers to prioritise mental health and well-being and encourage members to take ownership in doing so as part of their entrepreneurial journey.

Access to Mental Health Resources
Entrepreneurs and small business owners should have access to affordable mental health resources, including therapy, counselling and support groups. Explore what is available through your doctor and make yourself aware of what else is available ensuring that these resources are readily accessible when you need them. Budget for your mental health support.

Work-Life Balance
Maintaining a healthy work-life balance is crucial for sustaining good mental health. Entrepreneurs should prioritise self-care, set boundaries around work hours however counter-intuitive that feels and *make* time for relaxation and leisure activities. Rest and recharging for a few hours can has a positive impact on your capacity to think and problem-solve.

Peer Support Networks
Building strong peer support networks can help entrepreneurs feel less isolated and provide valuable emotional support. Networking groups, mentorship programs, and entrepreneur communities can offer a sense of belonging and camaraderie.

Financial Planning and Support
Having access to financial planning resources and support can help alleviate some of the stress associated with financial insecurity. This may include access to small business loans, grants, or financial counselling services. Make enquiries and have people in place so you can call on them when you need them.

Education and Training

This book exists so that you are able to educate yourself about the importance of mental health and stress management techniques that can help you recognise warning signs and develop coping strategies. This could be integrated into entrepreneurship education programs, workshops and seminars.

Promote a Healthy Workplace Culture

For entrepreneurs with employees, modelling (practice what you preach) and fostering a healthy workplace culture that prioritises employee well-being can have a positive impact on mental health. This includes offering benefits such as paid time off, flexible work arrangements, and mental health support services.

Suicide rates vary significantly from country to country and are influenced by numerous factors such as cultural norms, access to mental health services, socioeconomic conditions, and more. This general overview is based on data available up to 2022:

Global Trends

According to the World Health Organisation (WHO), suicide is the 17th leading cause of death worldwide. Suicide rates vary by region. For example, countries in Eastern Europe, particularly Lithuania, Russia, and Belarus, have historically had some of the highest suicide rates in the world. Similarly, countries in Southeast Asia, such as Sri Lanka and India also experience significant suicide rates.

Pandemic Impact

The COVID-19 pandemic has raised concerns about its impact on mental health and suicide rates. While data specific to the pandemic's effect on suicide rates is still being analysed, there have been reports of increased mental health challenges, including anxiety, depression and suicidal ideation, due to factors such as social isolation, economic uncertainty and disruption of mental health services.

High-Risk Groups

Certain populations may be at higher risk of suicide, including individuals with mental health disorders, LGBTQ+ individuals facing discrimination and stigma, veterans experiencing post-traumatic stress disorder (PTSD) and marginalised communities facing socioeconomic disparities.

Summary

It's essential to interpret suicide statistics with caution, as reporting practices, cultural attitudes toward suicide and data collection methods can vary widely between countries. Additionally, suicide is a complex issue influenced and informed by numerous factors and addressing it effectively requires a multifaceted approach that considers both individual and societal factors.

By addressing these factors and implementing strategies to support the mental health and well-being of entrepreneurs and small business owners, we can work towards reducing the incidence of suicide within this community and creating a more supportive and sustainable entrepreneurial ecosystem.

If you feel at risk of harm now, please contact the:

Samaritans in the UK on 116 123

Or 988 in the USA

Or contact your GP or Family doctor, or call an ambulance and ask for support.

Remember these feelings come *and* go and you won't feel like this forever. Seeking therapeutic support and processing emotions can help alleviate symptoms and teach you strategies to help you cope

Self Reflection Questions:
1. Reflect on a recent challenge or setback you've faced. How did you initially respond to it, and how did you ultimately overcome it?
2. Describe a time when you felt overwhelmed or stressed. What coping mechanisms did you use to manage your stress, and were they effective?
3. Identify three of your core values or beliefs. How do these values influence your decisions and actions in your daily life?
4. Explore a goal or aspiration you have for yourself. What steps can you take to move closer to achieving this goal, and how can you hold yourself accountable?
5. Consider a negative thought pattern or self-limiting belief you often experience. How does this thought pattern impact your self-esteem and

Chapter 15: Entrepreneurs and Suicide

behaviour, and what strategies can you use to challenge and reframe it?

6. Reflect on a time when you received constructive criticism or feedback. How did you react to it initially, and what did you learn from the experience?
7. Describe a recent situation in which you felt grateful or appreciative. How did expressing gratitude impact your mood and overall well-being?
8. Explore a hobby or activity that brings you joy or fulfilment. How can you incorporate more of this activity into your daily routine to enhance your happiness?
9. Reflect on your relationships with friends, family, or colleagues. Are there any boundaries you need to set or communication skills you can improve to strengthen these relationships?
10. Consider a time when you experienced failure or disappointment. What lessons did you learn from the experience, and how did it contribute to your personal growth?
11. Identify one small, achievable goal you can set for yourself this week to prioritize self-care. How will you ensure you follow through on this goal?
12. Reflect on your current stressors and sources of anxiety. What strategies can you implement to better manage stress and promote relaxation in your daily life?

13. Explore your support network and the people you can turn to during difficult times. How can you nurture these relationships and express gratitude for their support?
14. Consider the role of physical activity and nutrition in your overall well-being. What small changes can you make to prioritize your physical health and energy levels?
15. Reflect on the concept of self-compassion and how you can cultivate a kinder, more forgiving attitude toward yourself during times of struggle or failure.

Bibliography and Suggested Reading:

1. Bering, J. (2011). The Belief Instinct: The Psychology of Souls, Destiny, and the Meaning of Life. Random House.
2. Brown, B. (2010). The Gifts of Imperfection: Let Go of Who You Think You're Supposed to Be and Embrace Who You Are. Hazelden Publishing.
3. Brown, B. (2012). Daring Greatly: How the Courage to Be Vulnerable Transforms the Way We Live, Love, Parent, and Lead. Avery.
4. Clear, J. (2018). Atomic Habits: An Easy & Proven Way to Build Good Habits & Break Bad Ones. Penguin Random House.
5. Goleman, D. (1995). Emotional Intelligence: Why It Can Matter More Than IQ. Bantam Books.
6. Glashoff, U. (2006). Let Me Finish. HarperCollins.
7. Glashoff, U. (2021). Why We Believe: Evolution and the Human Way of Being. Simon & Schuster.
8. Gutkind, L. (Ed.). (2013). I Wasn't Strong Like This When I Started Out: True Stories of Becoming a Nurse. In Fact Books.
9. Haig, M. (2015). Reasons to Stay Alive. Canongate Books.
10. Hecht, J. M. (2013). Stay: A History of Suicide and the Arguments Against It. Yale University Press.
11. Jeffers, S. (1987). Feel the Fear . . . and Do It Anyway. Ballantine Books.
12. Lukach, M. (2017). My Lovely Wife in the Psych Ward: A Memoir. HarperCollins.
13. Sincero, J. (2013). You Are a Badass: How to Stop Doubting Your Greatness and Start Living an Awesome Life. Running Press.
14. Tolle, E. (1997). The Power of Now: A Guide to Spiritual Enlightenment. New World Library.

Chapter 15: Entrepreneurs and Suicide

15. Unknown. (2012). The Lost Art of Sinking: A Memoir of My Near-Death Experiences. HarperCollins.
16. Unknown. (2021). A Very Human Ending: How Suicide Haunts Our Species. HarperCollins.

Chapter 16: Sustaining Success: The Journey Never Ends

Success isn't a one-time accomplishment but an ongoing journey. It demands perpetual effort, adaptation, and growth to uphold. In this chapter, we'll delve into strategies for embracing the continuous journey of personal and professional development, prioritising well-being amidst success, and fostering a mindset of lifelong learning and growth. Some of the most successful people in the world have also experienced failure and used it to leverage their growth.

Embracing the Continuous Journey

Success is often misconstrued as reaching a static endpoint. However, genuine success lies in embracing the journey itself. Dweck (2006) reveals the significance of adopting a growth mindset; a belief that abilities and intelligence *can* be developed through dedication and perseverance. Individuals with a growth mindset are more resilient in the face of challenges and tend to embrace lifelong learning.

Case Study: The Growth Mindset in Action

Consider the journey of Michael Jordan, widely regarded as one of the greatest basketball players of all time. Despite facing numerous setbacks early in his career, Jordan's unwavering commitment to improvement and his belief in the power of hard work propelled him to unparalleled success. His dedication to continuous growth exemplifies the essence of a growth mindset.

Strategies for Maintaining Well-being Amidst Success

Success can sometimes come at the expense of well-being if not managed effectively. Long hours, chronic stress and neglecting self-care can lead to burnout and decreased satisfaction. Therefore, it's imperative to prioritise well-being even amidst achievement.

Csikszentmihalyi (1990) emphasises the concept of 'flow'; a state of complete immersion and focus in an activity. Cultivating hobbies, practicing mindfulness, and establishing boundaries between work and personal life can all contribute to maintaining well-being amidst success. Rest as we have discussed throughout this book is a necessary and essential component of well-being.

Case Study: Prioritising Well-being

'We need to accept that we won't always make the right decisions, that we'll screw up royally sometimes; *understanding* that failure is not the opposite of success, it's part of success.'

Arianna Huffington

Let's examine the approach taken by Arianna Huffington, co-founder of The Huffington Post. Following a personal experience with burnout, Huffington became a vocal advocate for prioritising well-being. She introduced initiatives such as nap rooms and meditation classes at The Huffington Post offices, recognising the importance of nurturing employee wellness alongside professional success.

Cultivating a Mindset of Lifelong Learning and Growth
In today's dynamic world, static knowledge and skills quickly become obsolete. Therefore, cultivating a mindset of lifelong learning and growth is essential for sustained success.

The role of deliberate practice, structured, focused efforts to improve performance in achieving mastery had been highlighted by Ericsson et al (1993). By actively seeking opportunities for learning and skill development, individuals can adapt to new challenges and remain competitive and refreshed.

Dr. Maya Angelou: A Testament to Lifelong Learning and Overcoming Trauma

'You may not control all the events that happen to you, but you *can* decide not to be reduced by them.'
Dr Maya Angelou

Dr. Maya Angelou's life story serves as a powerful testament to the importance of lifelong learning and resilience in the face of adversity. Despite enduring a traumatic childhood marked by racial discrimination, sexual abuse and familial instability, Dr Angelou refused to be defined by her circumstances. Instead, she embraced a journey of continuous growth and self-discovery. Through her literary works, including the iconic autobiography 'I Know Why the Caged Bird Sings,' Dr Angelou shared her harrowing experiences with honesty and vulnerability, inspiring countless individuals to confront their own challenges with courage and determination.

Dr Angelou's commitment to lifelong learning was evident throughout her life as she pursued diverse interests, including writing, acting, activism and teaching. She understood that true growth comes from embracing new experiences and perspectives, even in the face of adversity and her experiences with imposter syndrome. Relentless resilience combined with Dr Angelou's unwavering belief in the power of education serve as a beacon of hope for those navigating their own journeys of healing and self-discovery. Her legacy reminds us that with perseverance and a thirst for knowledge, we can overcome even the most daunting obstacles and achieve greatness.

Individual Responsibility and Autonomy
While external factors undoubtedly influence success, individuals also bear responsibility for their own growth and development. Taking ownership of one's actions and decisions is paramount for sustained success of any individual.

Bandura (1977) underscored the importance of self-efficacy: the belief in one's ability to achieve goals and overcome obstacles. Individuals with high self-efficacy are more likely to set ambitious goals, persist in the face of adversity and ultimately succeed.

Chapter 16: Sustaining Success: The Journey Never Ends

President Nelson Mandela: A Beacon of Lifelong Learning and Resilience

> 'Do not judge me by my successes, judge me by how many times I fell down and got back up again.'
>
> President Nelson Mandela

President Nelson Mandela's, (lovingly and respectfully referred to as Madiba), life exemplifies the transformative power of lifelong learning and resilience in the face of profound adversity. Born into a racially divided South Africa, Madiba faced systemic oppression and injustice from an early age. Despite enduring decades of imprisonment and harsh persecution for his anti-apartheid activism, Madiba remained steadfast in his commitment to justice, equality, forgiveness and reconciliation.

Throughout his life, Madiba embraced learning as a tool for personal and societal transformation. Despite being denied a formal education during his youth due to apartheid policies, Madiba pursued knowledge through self-study and engagement with fellow political prisoners. His time in prison became a crucible for intellectual growth, as he devoured books on philosophy, politics, and history, deepening his understanding of the world and refining his vision for a democratic South Africa.

Madiba's commitment to education extended beyond his own personal development. Upon his release from prison in 1990, he dedicated himself to building a more inclusive and equitable society through education and lifelong learning initiatives. As South Africa's first black president, Madiba prioritised education as a fundamental right and a bedrock of nation-building. He launched initiatives to expand access to schooling for all children, eradicate illiteracy and promote adult education, recognising the transformative potential of knowledge to uplift individuals and communities.

President Mandela's resilience in the face of adversity and his unwavering commitment to justice and reconciliation continue to inspire people around the world. His lifelong pursuit of learning and his belief in the power of education as a catalyst for social change are enduring legacies that remind us of the importance of intellectual curiosity, resilience, and lifelong learning in the pursuit of a more just and equitable world. As Madiba himself once said, 'Education is the most powerful weapon which you can use to change the world.'

Case Study: Self-efficacy in Action - Oprah Winfrey

'The biggest adventure you can take is to live the life of your dreams.'
Oprah Winfrey

Oprah Winfrey's life is a compelling example of how self-efficacy- the belief in one's ability to achieve goals, can drive remarkable success, even in the face of formidable obstacles. Born into poverty in rural Mississippi, Winfrey experienced a tumultuous childhood marked by poverty, abuse, rejection and instability. Despite these early challenges, she possessed an unwavering belief in her own potential and a relentless determination to create a better life for herself.

From a young age, Winfrey demonstrated resilience and ambition. Despite enduring abuse and hardship, she

Chapter 16: Sustaining Success: The Journey Never Ends

excelled academically and showed a natural talent for public speaking and storytelling. These early experiences instilled in her a sense of self-confidence and a belief that she could overcome adversity through hard work and perseverance.

As Winfrey pursued her career in media, she encountered numerous setbacks and obstacles. Early in her broadcasting career, she faced discrimination and scepticism from industry professionals who doubted her ability to succeed as a black woman in a predominantly white, male-dominated field. However, Winfrey refused to be deterred by these challenges. Instead, she remained steadfast in her belief in her own abilities and persisted in pursuing her dreams.

Winfrey's breakthrough came with the launch of her groundbreaking talk show, 'The Oprah Winfrey Show,' in 1986. Despite initial doubts and low ratings, Winfrey's authenticity, empathy, courage and genuine connection with her audience resonated deeply, catapulting her to unprecedented levels of success and influence. Over the course of its 25-year run, 'The Oprah Winfrey Show' became the highest-rated talk show in television history, reaching millions of viewers worldwide and transforming Winfrey into a cultural icon.

Beyond her achievements in media, Winfrey has leveraged her platform for positive social change, using her influence to advocate for causes such as education, empowerment, and wellness. Through her philanthropic efforts, including the establishment of the Oprah Winfrey Leadership

Academy for Girls in South Africa, Winfrey has empowered countless individuals to pursue their dreams and overcome adversity.

Winfrey's remarkable success is a testament to the power of self-efficacy to overcome obstacles and achieve extraordinary goals. Despite facing significant adversity in her early life and in her professional career, she never wavered in her belief in her own potential. Instead, she embraced challenges as opportunities for growth and leveraged her strengths to create a legacy of impact and inspiration. Winfrey's story serves as a powerful reminder that with self-belief, resilience, and determination, anything is possible.

Summary

Success is not a destination but a continuous journey of growth and development. By embracing this journey, prioritising well-being, cultivating a mindset of lifelong learning, and taking ownership of one's actions, individuals can sustain success in the long term. The journey of success is ongoing, it's up to each individual to navigate it with resilience, determination, and a commitment to growth knowing without doubt, that giving our very best at any given time *is* enough.

Self Reflection Questions
1. Reflect on a recent success in your life. How can you leverage this success to fuel further growth and development?
2. What strategies do you currently employ to maintain well-being amidst your pursuit of success?

How can you enhance these strategies to better support your overall well-being?
3. How do you approach learning and skill development in your personal or professional life? Identify areas where you could adopt a more deliberate and proactive approach to learning.
4. Recall a time when you faced a significant challenge or setback. How did you respond, and what did you learn from the experience? How can you apply these lessons to future endeavours?

Bibliography

1. Bandura, A. (1977). Self-efficacy: Toward a unifying theory of behavioural change. Psychological Review, 84(2), 191–215.
2. Duckworth, A. L., & Seligman, M. E. P. (2005). Self-discipline outdoes IQ in predicting academic performance of adolescents. Psychological Science, 16(12), 939–944.
3. Duhigg, C. (2012). The Power of Habit: Why We Do What We Do in Life and Business. Random House.
4. Ericsson, K. A., Krampe, R. T., & Tesch-Römer, C. (1993). The role of deliberate practice in the acquisition of expert performance. Psychological Review, 100(3), 363–406.

Further Reading

1. Angelou, M. (1969). I Know Why the Caged Bird Sings. Random House.
2. Brown, B. (2012). Daring Greatly: How the Courage to Be Vulnerable Transforms the Way We Live, Love, Parent, and Lead. Avery.
3. Cain, S. (2013). Quiet: The Power of Introverts in a World That Can't Stop Talking. Broadway Books
4. Csikszentmihalyi, M. (1990). Flow: The Psychology of Optimal Experience. Harper & Row.
5. Dweck, C. S. (2006). Mindset: The New Psychology of Success. Random House.
6. Duckworth, A. L. (2016). Grit: The Power of Passion and Perseverance. Scribner.
7. Frankl, V. E. (1946). Man's Search for Meaning. Beacon Press.
8. Gladwell, M. (2008). Outliers: The Story of Success. Little, Brown and Company.

9. Grant, A. (2013). Give and Take: A Revolutionary Approach to Success. Penguin Books.
10. Mandela, N. (1994). Long Walk to Freedom. Little, Brown and Company.
11. Newport, C. (2016). Deep Work: Rules for Focused Success in a Distracted World. Grand Central Publishing.
12. Pink, D. H. (2009). Drive: The Surprising Truth About What Motivates Us. Riverhead Books.
13. Sinek, S. (2011). Start with Why: How Great Leaders Inspire Everyone to Take Action. Portfoli

About the Author:

Bhavna talks passionately about Mental Health and Wellbeing working with Leadership, HR advisors and Employees, the lifeblood of every organisation. Bhavna has helped leaders and organisations around the world to address their Wellbeing strategies by creating inclusive, respectful, psychologically safe, happy and nurturing environments where both employees *and* the company can thrive.

From her work as an accredited Psychotherapist, Coach, International Keynote Speaker, Supervisor, Author, Critical Incident Debriefer Trainer and Educator with 30 years' experience, Bhavna has supported over 19k clients globally with professional help. She has supported managers and organisations to bring dignity, empathy, allyship and compassion back into the workplace as well as reduce the impact on Mental Health from racism and discrimination towards the BAME and LGBTQ+ Community.

Bhavna was part of the **UN Women's CW68 UK Delegation** in 2024 where she virtually shared her input with women leaders from around the world meeting at the UN Headquarters in New York on the topic of **Women and Girls' Rights** and the need for financial equality.

Bhavna's work with multi-billion $ business clients including major Police Forces, National Retail and Manufacturing Industry chains in the UK, Europe, Asia and Americas places emphasis on employee Well-Being strategies and Creating Better Organisational Cultures through Allyship.

Bhavna frequently guests on Radio, international podcasts and speaks at conferences sharing lessons from her personal Coming Out journey especially as an academically accomplished Indian Woman, in a frequently exclusive field. She has been an invited speaker on webinars and panels discussing Mental Health, Suicide and Relationships as well as Championing LGBTQ+ Employee Mental Health and Well-Being locally and internationally.

She has been commissioned as an Expert Guest Author to write articles in seven issues on Stress, LGBTQ+ issues, Mental Health, Journalling, Bullying, Grief and Coming Out in Later Life for Happiful, a leading Mental Health magazine and as a contributor for Hello! Magazine on an article commissioned after news of King Charles' cancer diagnosis was released. She is a regular contributor to the BACP's resource library of articles and educational videos for the public covering Mental Health, Stress and LGBTQ+ issues.

In her spare time, Bhavna's passions include writing, playing with fountain pens and inks, she has been an Ink Tester for UK's largest and oldest Ink manufacturer. Her other self-care passions include rewatching Jurassic Park movies, audiobooks, long walks and snail mail. Being a

About the Author:

foodie, she enjoys vegetarian cuisine especially dosa, samosa, eggless cake and copious amounts of chai.

To book Bhavna to speak at your:

Conference, **Organisation**, to **Leadership**, **ERG** groups and **Pride** events please get in touch via:

www.justbeyourself.co.uk
email: bhavnaraithathaconsultancy@outlook.com

Also by Bhavna Raithatha

Get The Set On Amazon

Bhavna Raithatha Consultancy

Both books are now available on Amazon Worldwide:

Paperback
Hardback
Ebook

I very much hope you have found this book of great value. Please consider leaving a review and share your thoughts and what you found most helpful.

I would be *delighted* to read your Amazon reviews and hear your feedback as a new author.

Warmest regards,

Bhavna

Notes

Notes

Notes

Driven: The Audacity to Thrive in Entrepreneurship

Printed in Great Britain
by Amazon